My First Book About Genetics

Donald M. Silver &
Patricia J. Wynne

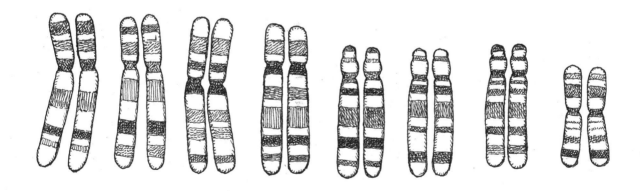

DOVER PUBLICATIONS, INC.

Mineola, New York

For Eli Sanchez . . .

Who packed three complicated lifetimes into 42 years.

Who was Gregor Mendel? What is genetics? How do genes pass along traits from one generation to another? You'll find out the answers to these and many more important questions in this fantastic coloring book! Easy-to-understand captions explain the basics of genetics and its importance in human, animal, and plant life. Discover the roles played by DNA and RNA as well as how genes protect you from illness, why nearly all calico cats are females, how genes determine the size and shape of the parts of a flower, and more. Plus, you can color each of the amazingly realistic illustrations using colored pencils, crayons, or markers.

Bibliographical Note
My First Book About Genetics is a new work,
first published by Dover Publications, Inc., in 2020.

International Standard Book Number
ISBN-13: 978-0-486-84047-5
ISBN-10: 0-486-84047-6

Manufactured in the United States by LSC Communications
84047601
www.doverpublications.com
2 4 6 8 10 9 7 5 3 1
2020

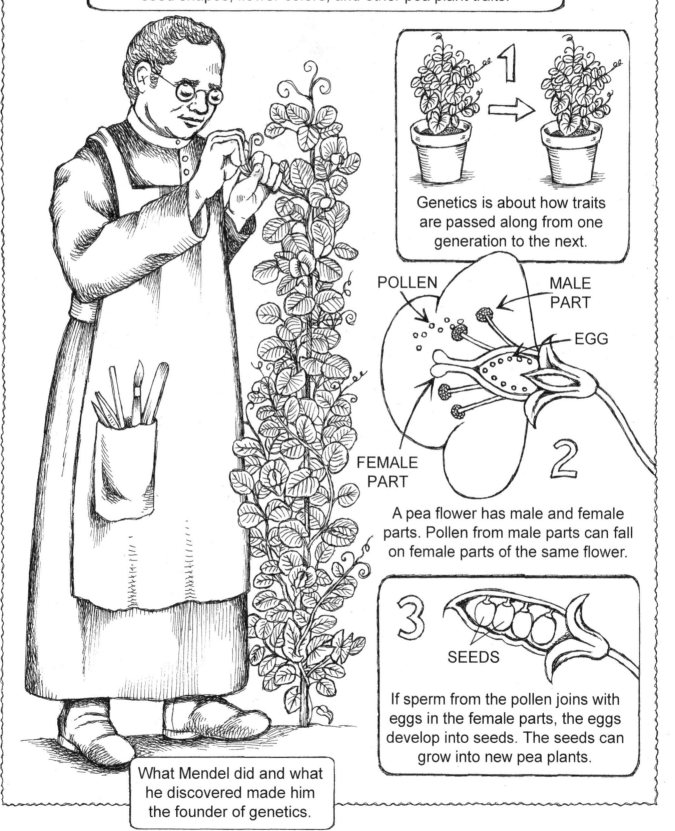

IN THE GARDEN
In 1854, the science of genetics began in a garden where Gregor Mendel grew pea plants. He wanted to study seed colors, seed shapes, flower colors, and other pea plant traits.

Genetics is about how traits are passed along from one generation to the next.

POLLEN

MALE PART

EGG

FEMALE PART

2

A pea flower has male and female parts. Pollen from male parts can fall on female parts of the same flower.

3

SEEDS

If sperm from the pollen joins with eggs in the female parts, the eggs develop into seeds. The seeds can grow into new pea plants.

What Mendel did and what he discovered made him the founder of genetics.

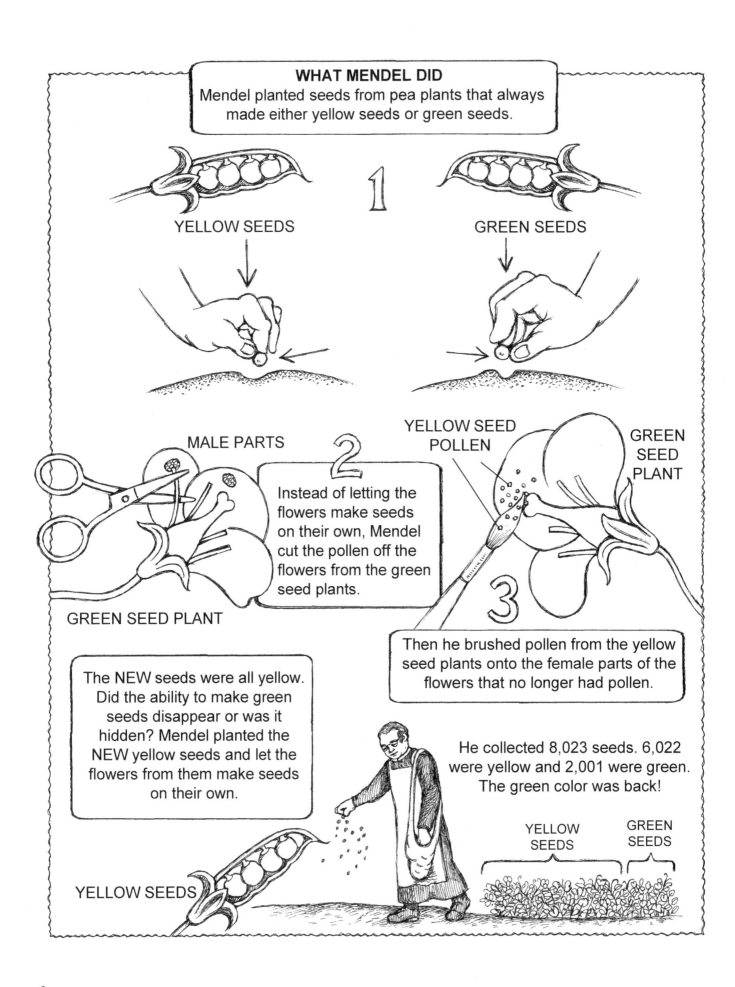

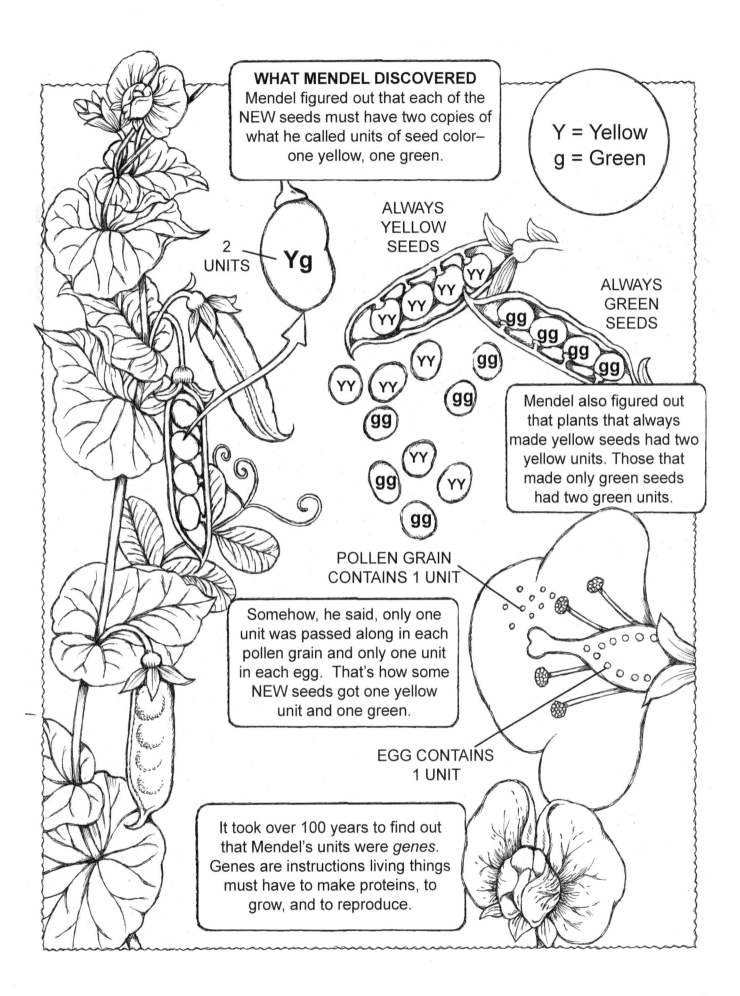

WHAT MENDEL DISCOVERED
Mendel figured out that each of the NEW seeds must have two copies of what he called units of seed color– one yellow, one green.

Y = Yellow
g = Green

2 UNITS — **Yg**

ALWAYS YELLOW SEEDS

ALWAYS GREEN SEEDS

Mendel also figured out that plants that always made yellow seeds had two yellow units. Those that made only green seeds had two green units.

POLLEN GRAIN CONTAINS 1 UNIT

Somehow, he said, only one unit was passed along in each pollen grain and only one unit in each egg. That's how some NEW seeds got one yellow unit and one green.

EGG CONTAINS 1 UNIT

It took over 100 years to find out that Mendel's units were *genes*. Genes are instructions living things must have to make proteins, to grow, and to reproduce.

3

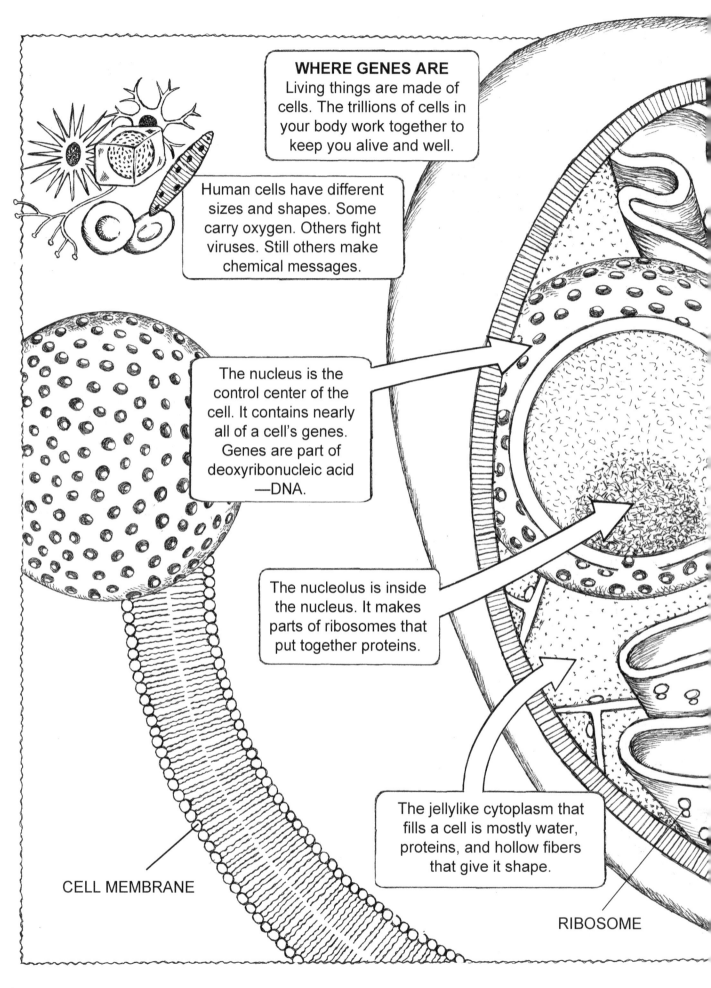

WHERE GENES ARE
Living things are made of cells. The trillions of cells in your body work together to keep you alive and well.

Human cells have different sizes and shapes. Some carry oxygen. Others fight viruses. Still others make chemical messages.

The nucleus is the control center of the cell. It contains nearly all of a cell's genes. Genes are part of deoxyribonucleic acid —DNA.

The nucleolus is inside the nucleus. It makes parts of ribosomes that put together proteins.

The jellylike cytoplasm that fills a cell is mostly water, proteins, and hollow fibers that give it shape.

CELL MEMBRANE

RIBOSOME

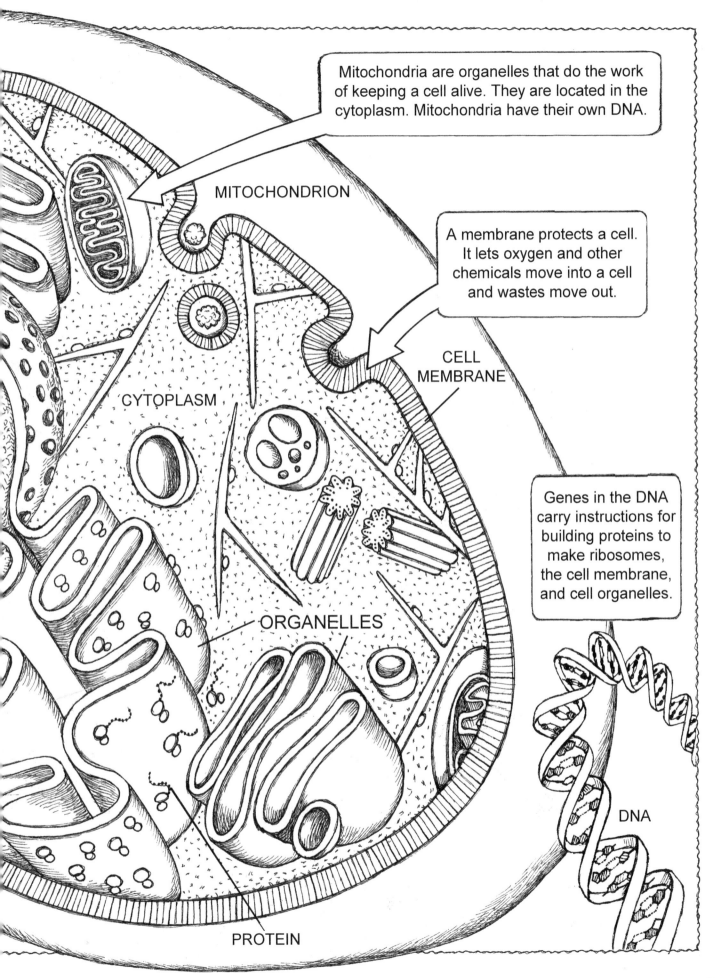

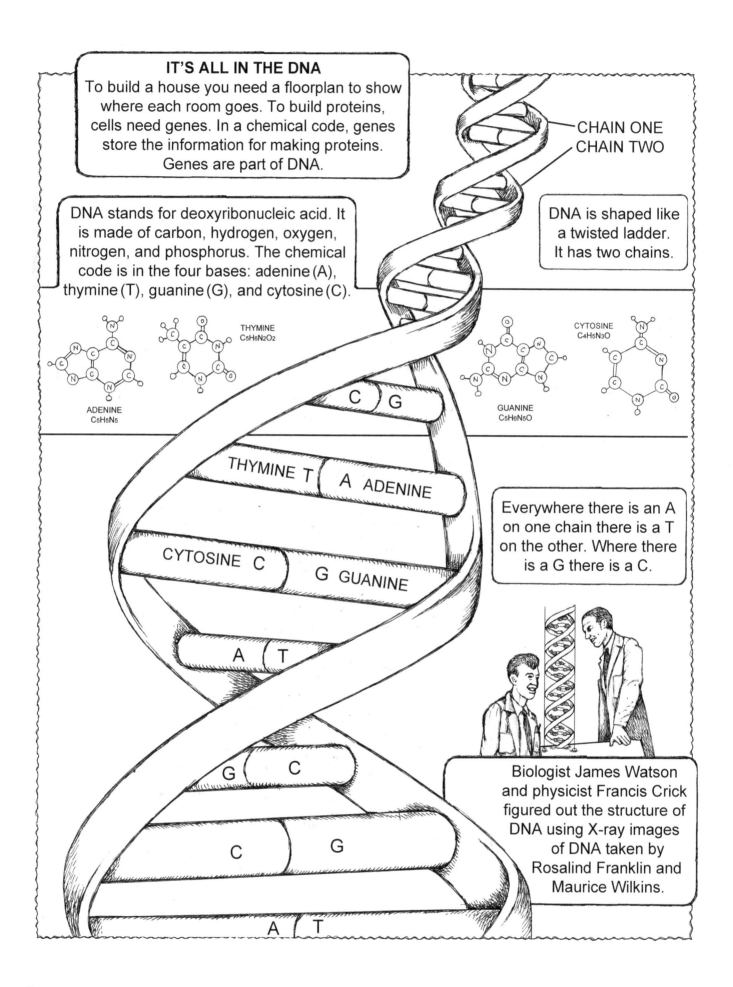

IT'S ALL IN THE DNA
To build a house you need a floorplan to show where each room goes. To build proteins, cells need genes. In a chemical code, genes store the information for making proteins. Genes are part of DNA.

CHAIN ONE
CHAIN TWO

DNA stands for deoxyribonucleic acid. It is made of carbon, hydrogen, oxygen, nitrogen, and phosphorus. The chemical code is in the four bases: adenine (A), thymine (T), guanine (G), and cytosine (C).

DNA is shaped like a twisted ladder. It has two chains.

THYMINE
$C_5H_6N_2O_2$

CYTOSINE
$C_4H_5N_3O$

ADENINE
$C_5H_5N_5$

GUANINE
$C_5H_6N_5O$

C G

THYMINE T   A ADENINE

Everywhere there is an A on one chain there is a T on the other. Where there is a G there is a C.

CYTOSINE C   G GUANINE

A T

Biologist James Watson and physicist Francis Crick figured out the structure of DNA using X-ray images of DNA taken by Rosalind Franklin and Maurice Wilkins.

G C

C G

A T

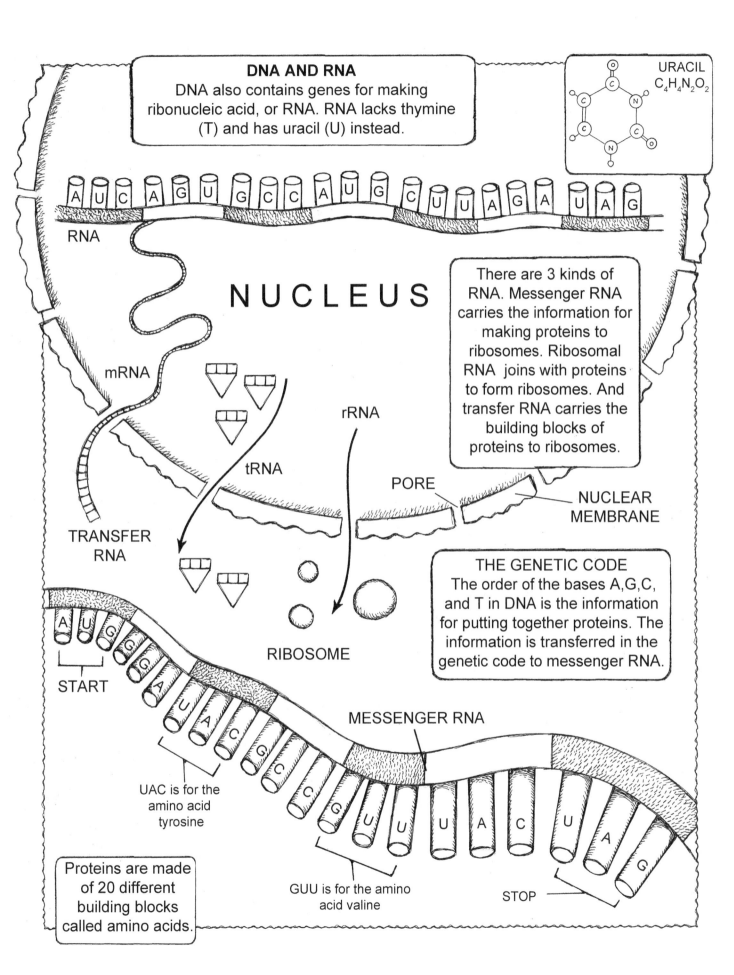

DNA AND RNA
DNA also contains genes for making ribonucleic acid, or RNA. RNA lacks thymine (T) and has uracil (U) instead.

URACIL
$C_4H_4N_2O_2$

RNA

NUCLEUS

mRNA

rRNA

There are 3 kinds of RNA. Messenger RNA carries the information for making proteins to ribosomes. Ribosomal RNA joins with proteins to form ribosomes. And transfer RNA carries the building blocks of proteins to ribosomes.

tRNA

PORE

NUCLEAR MEMBRANE

TRANSFER RNA

THE GENETIC CODE
The order of the bases A,G,C, and T in DNA is the information for putting together proteins. The information is transferred in the genetic code to messenger RNA.

RIBOSOME

START

MESSENGER RNA

UAC is for the amino acid tyrosine

Proteins are made of 20 different building blocks called amino acids.

GUU is for the amino acid valine

STOP

7

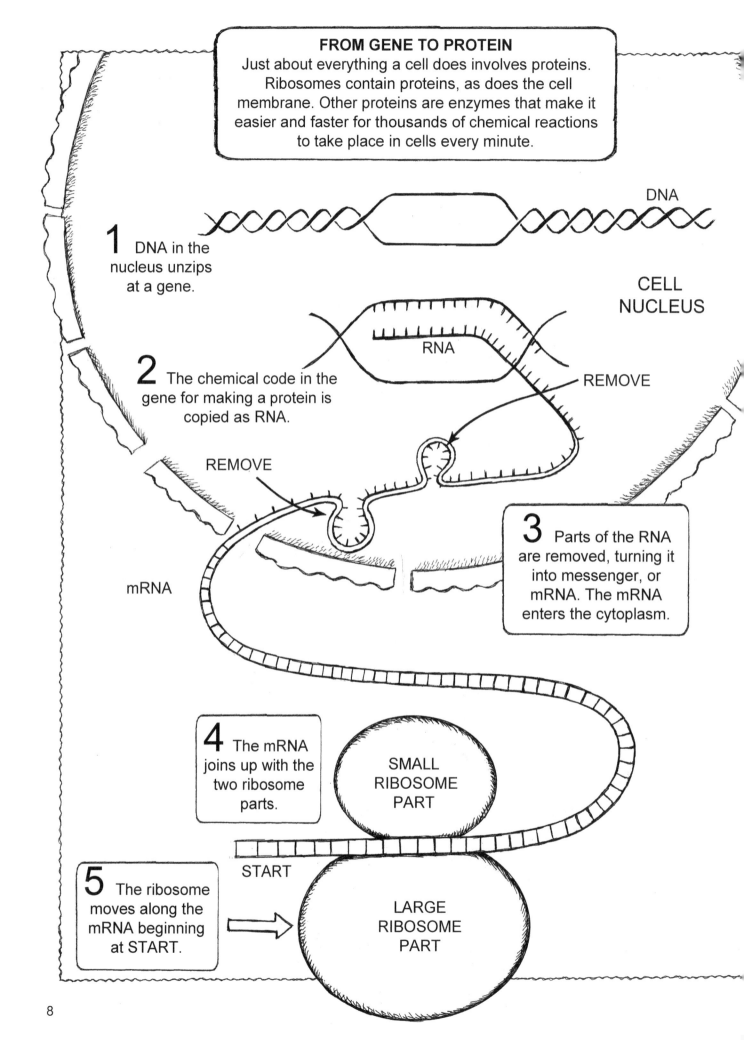

FROM GENE TO PROTEIN
Just about everything a cell does involves proteins.
Ribosomes contain proteins, as does the cell
membrane. Other proteins are enzymes that make it
easier and faster for thousands of chemical reactions
to take place in cells every minute.

DNA

1 DNA in the
nucleus unzips
at a gene.

CELL
NUCLEUS

RNA

2 The chemical code in the
gene for making a protein is
copied as RNA.

REMOVE

REMOVE

3 Parts of the RNA
are removed, turning it
into messenger, or
mRNA. The mRNA
enters the cytoplasm.

mRNA

4 The mRNA
joins up with the
two ribosome
parts.

SMALL
RIBOSOME
PART

START

5 The ribosome
moves along the
mRNA beginning
at START.

LARGE
RIBOSOME
PART

8

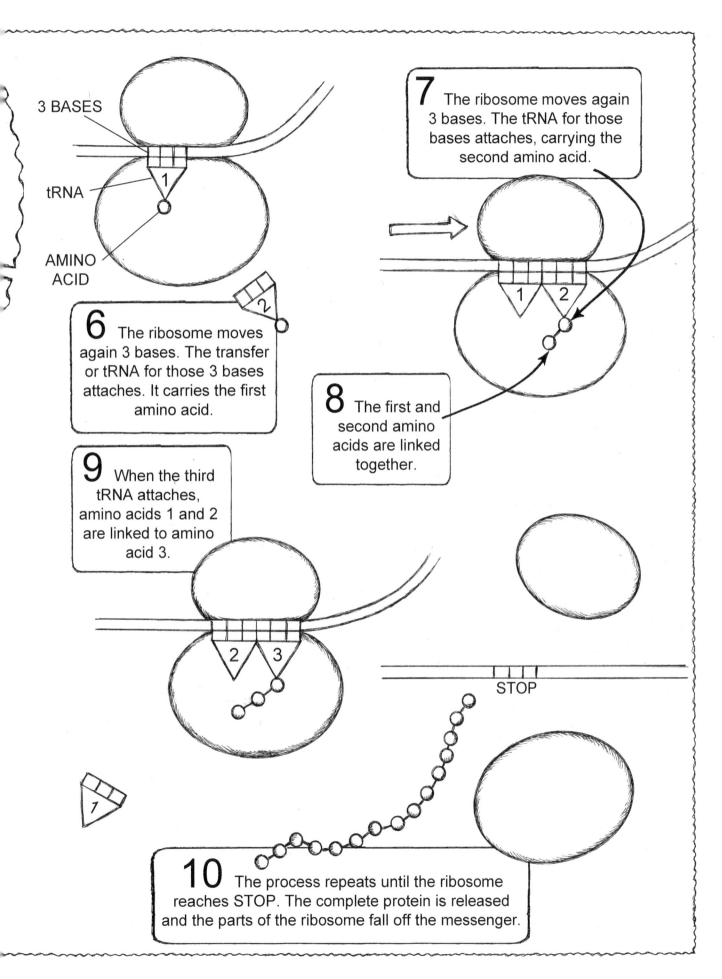

3 BASES

tRNA

AMINO ACID

6 The ribosome moves again 3 bases. The transfer or tRNA for those 3 bases attaches. It carries the first amino acid.

7 The ribosome moves again 3 bases. The tRNA for those bases attaches, carrying the second amino acid.

8 The first and second amino acids are linked together.

9 When the third tRNA attaches, amino acids 1 and 2 are linked to amino acid 3.

STOP

10 The process repeats until the ribosome reaches STOP. The complete protein is released and the parts of the ribosome fall off the messenger.

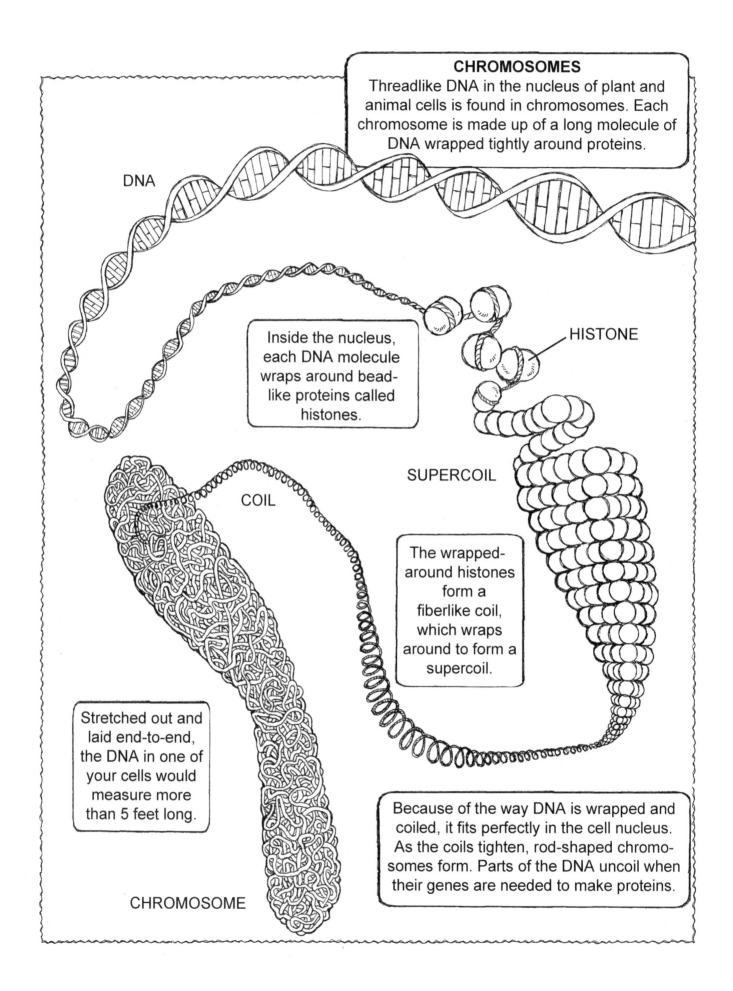

CHROMOSOMES
Threadlike DNA in the nucleus of plant and animal cells is found in chromosomes. Each chromosome is made up of a long molecule of DNA wrapped tightly around proteins.

DNA

HISTONE

Inside the nucleus, each DNA molecule wraps around bead-like proteins called histones.

SUPERCOIL

COIL

The wrapped-around histones form a fiberlike coil, which wraps around to form a supercoil.

Stretched out and laid end-to-end, the DNA in one of your cells would measure more than 5 feet long.

Because of the way DNA is wrapped and coiled, it fits perfectly in the cell nucleus. As the coils tighten, rod-shaped chromosomes form. Parts of the DNA uncoil when their genes are needed to make proteins.

CHROMOSOME

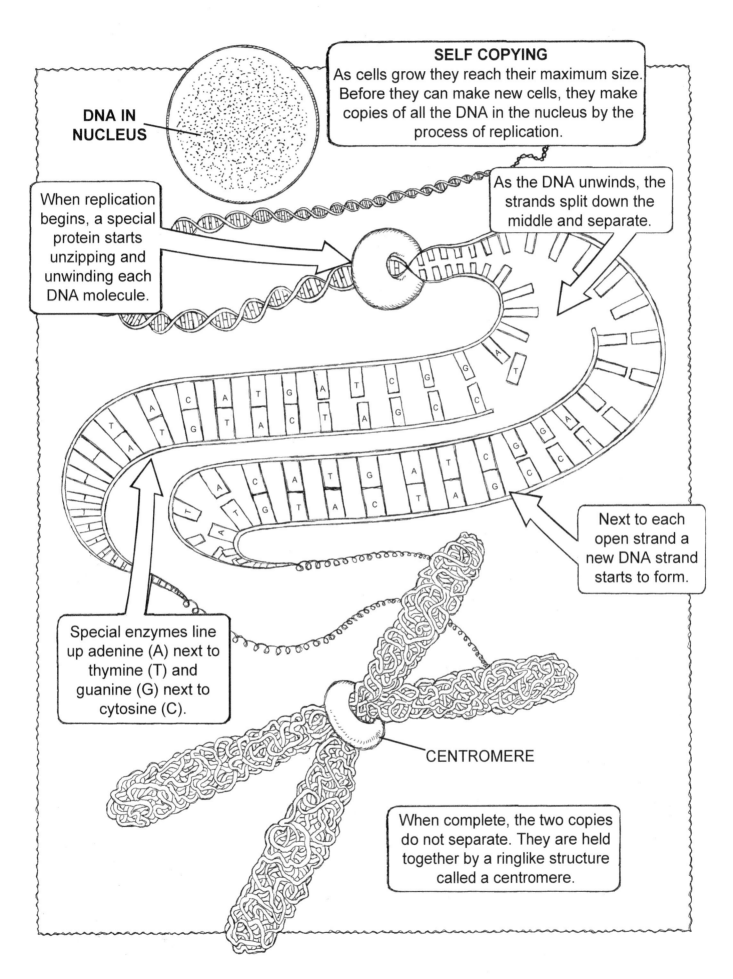

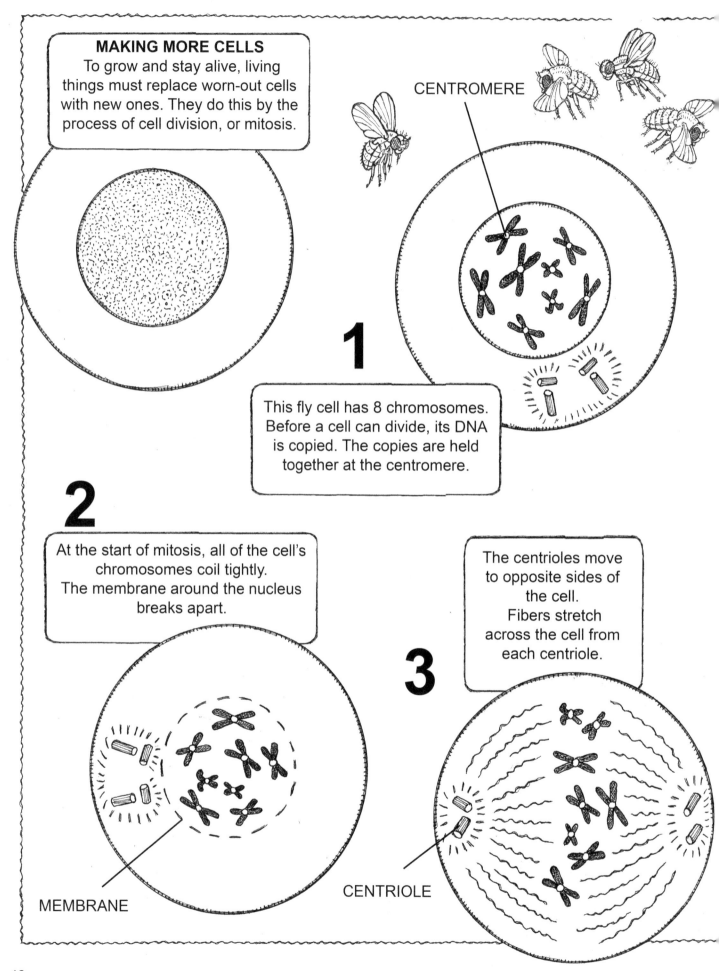

MAKING MORE CELLS
To grow and stay alive, living things must replace worn-out cells with new ones. They do this by the process of cell division, or mitosis.

CENTROMERE

1

This fly cell has 8 chromosomes. Before a cell can divide, its DNA is copied. The copies are held together at the centromere.

2

At the start of mitosis, all of the cell's chromosomes coil tightly.
The membrane around the nucleus breaks apart.

MEMBRANE

3

The centrioles move to opposite sides of the cell.
Fibers stretch across the cell from each centriole.

CENTRIOLE

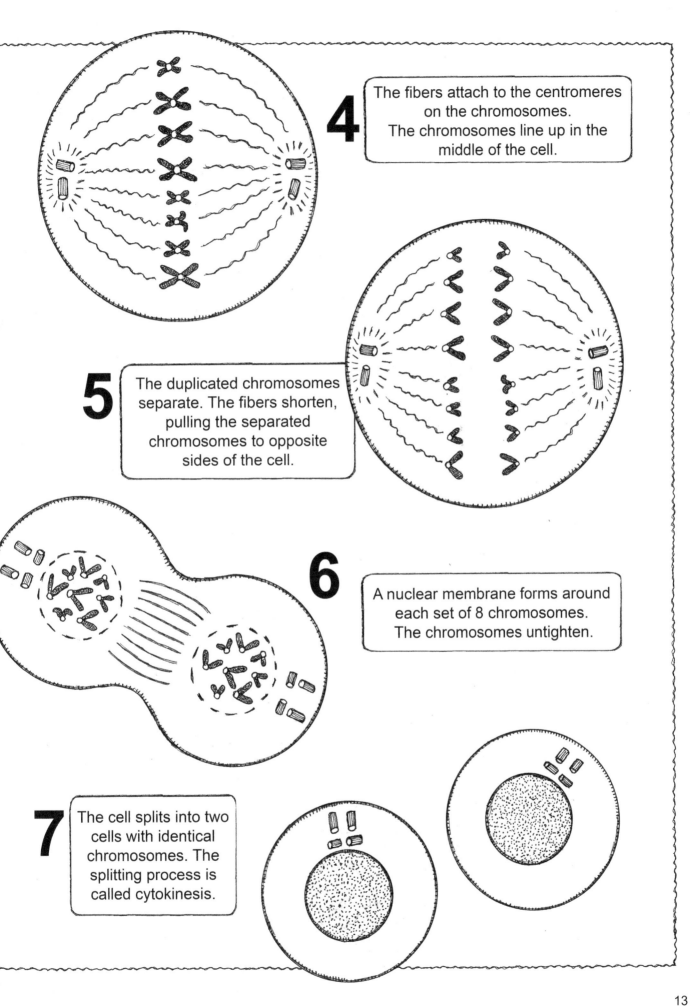

4 The fibers attach to the centromeres on the chromosomes. The chromosomes line up in the middle of the cell.

5 The duplicated chromosomes separate. The fibers shorten, pulling the separated chromosomes to opposite sides of the cell.

6 A nuclear membrane forms around each set of 8 chromosomes. The chromosomes untighten.

7 The cell splits into two cells with identical chromosomes. The splitting process is called cytokinesis.

13

THE COMPLETE SET
You have 46 chromosomes: 23 came from your father and 23 from your mother. For every chromosome from your father there is one from your mother.

A complete set of chromosomes is called a karyotype.

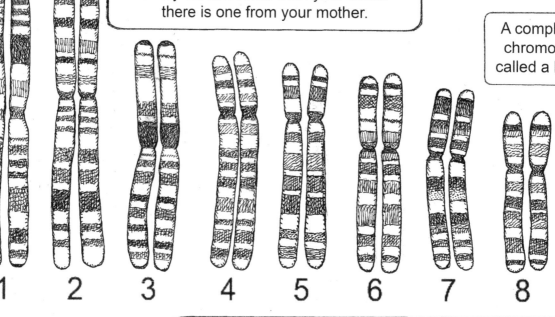

Scientists study tightly coiled duplicated chromosomes by staining them with colored chemicals. The chemicals turn different parts of the chromosomes into colored bands.

The chromosome pairs are numbered 1 to 22. Pair 23, the sex chromosomes, are XX for girls and XY for boys.

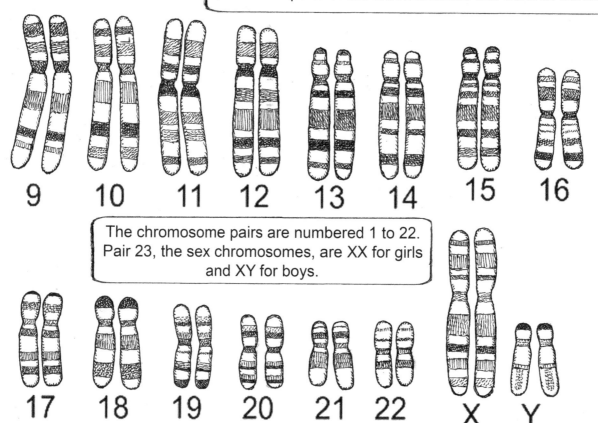

Dogs have 39 pairs, or 78 chromosomes.

1	2	3	4	5	6	7
8	9	10	11	12	13	14
15	16	17	18	19	20	21
22	23	24	25	26	27	28
29	30	31	32	33	34	35
36	37	38		X	Y	

COUNT ON THEM
Living things have different numbers of chromosomes with different numbers of genes on them.

Pea plants have 14 pairs, or 28 chromosomes.

Cats have 19 pairs, or 38 chromosomes.

Elephants have 28 pairs, or 56 chromosomes.

1	2	3	4	5	6
7	8	9	10	11	12
13	14	15	16	17	18
19	20	21	22	23	24
25	26	27			X X

Potatoes have 24 pairs, or 48 chromosomes.

1	2	3	4	5	6	7	8	9	10	11	12
13	14	15	16	17	18		19	20	21	22	23
24	25	26	27	28	29	30	31	32	33	34	35
36	37	38	39	40	41	42	43	44	45		46

Giant sequoia trees have 11 pairs, or 22 chromosomes.

Goldfish have 47 pairs, or 94 chromosomes.

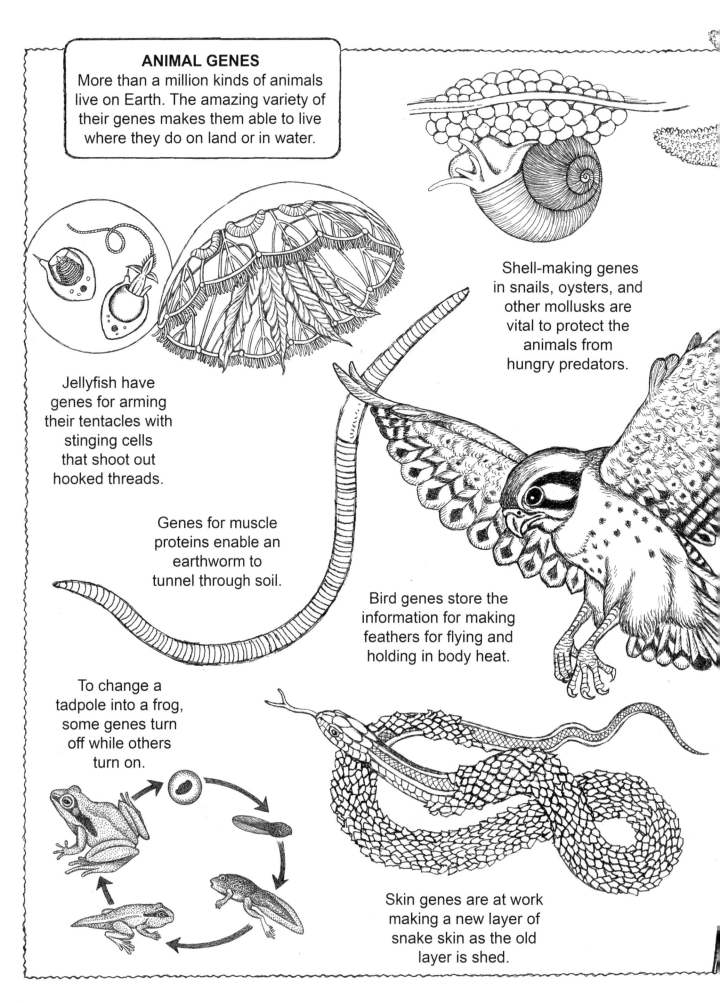

ANIMAL GENES
More than a million kinds of animals live on Earth. The amazing variety of their genes makes them able to live where they do on land or in water.

Shell-making genes in snails, oysters, and other mollusks are vital to protect the animals from hungry predators.

Jellyfish have genes for arming their tentacles with stinging cells that shoot out hooked threads.

Genes for muscle proteins enable an earthworm to tunnel through soil.

Bird genes store the information for making feathers for flying and holding in body heat.

To change a tadpole into a frog, some genes turn off while others turn on.

Skin genes are at work making a new layer of snake skin as the old layer is shed.

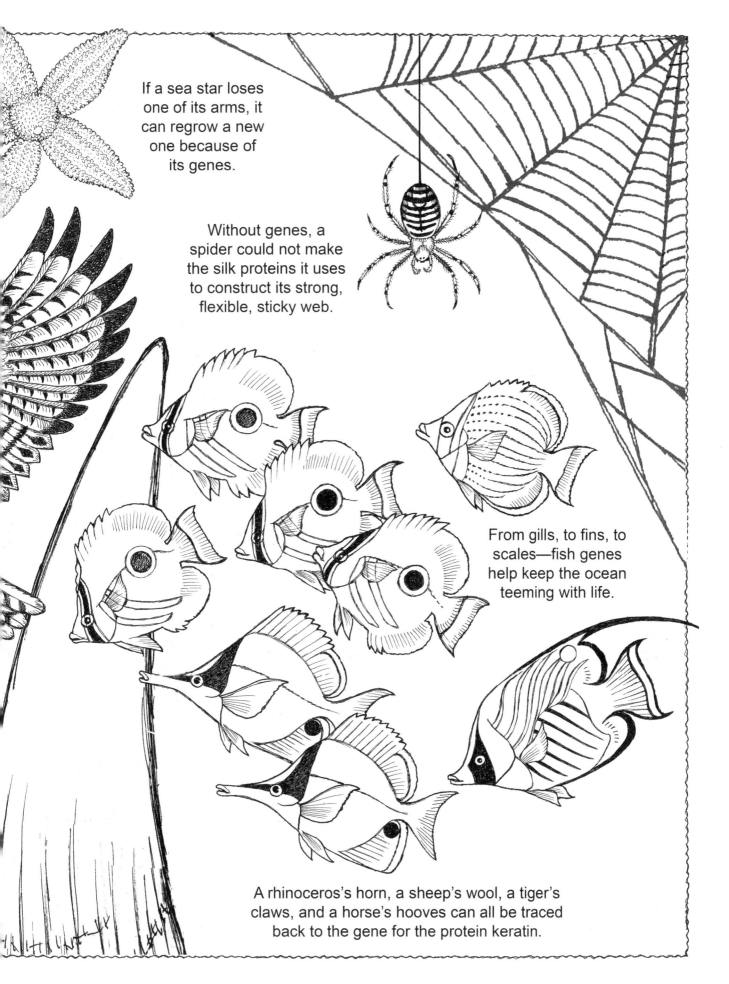

If a sea star loses one of its arms, it can regrow a new one because of its genes.

Without genes, a spider could not make the silk proteins it uses to construct its strong, flexible, sticky web.

From gills, to fins, to scales—fish genes help keep the ocean teeming with life.

A rhinoceros's horn, a sheep's wool, a tiger's claws, and a horse's hooves can all be traced back to the gene for the protein keratin.

PLANT GENES
The proteins coded for plant genes control everything plants do that animals can't: make food, grow flowers, form fruits, make wood, and much more.

Without genes for making chlorophyll, green leaves could not soak up energy from the sun and use it to make food by photosynthesis.

For leaves to turn colors in autumn, green chlorophyll must be broken down by special proteins.

Most cactuses rely on genes for making sharp spines that protect them from being eaten by animals.

The shape, color, and size of every flower part is under the control of many genes.

This frog, trapped by a Venus flytrap plant, will be digested by proteins and acid the plant gives off.

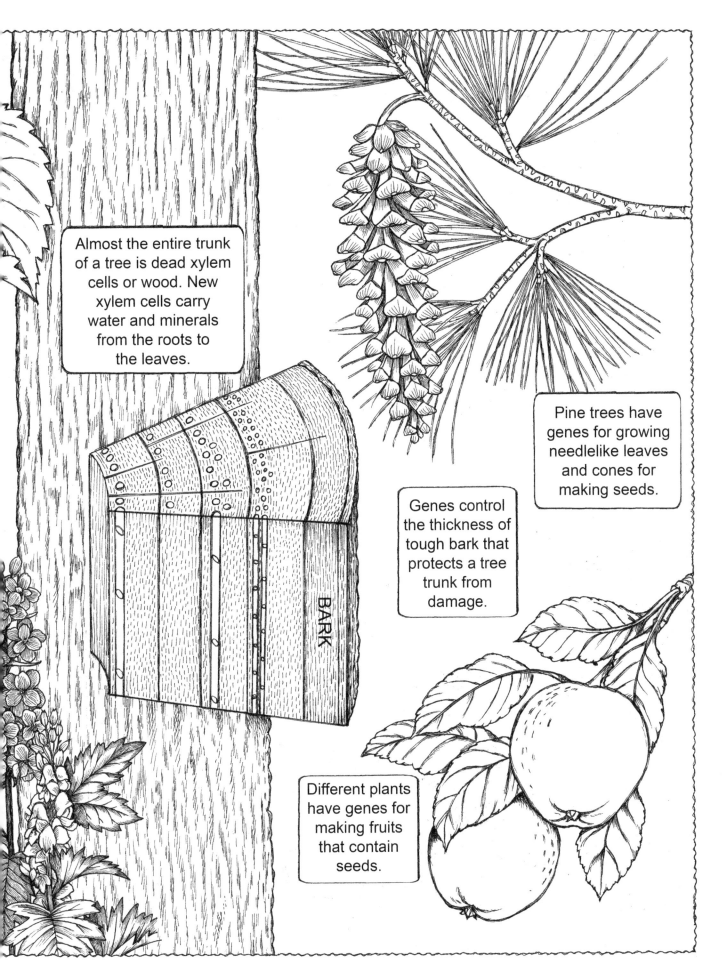

Almost the entire trunk of a tree is dead xylem cells or wood. New xylem cells carry water and minerals from the roots to the leaves.

Pine trees have genes for growing needlelike leaves and cones for making seeds.

Genes control the thickness of tough bark that protects a tree trunk from damage.

BARK

Different plants have genes for making fruits that contain seeds.

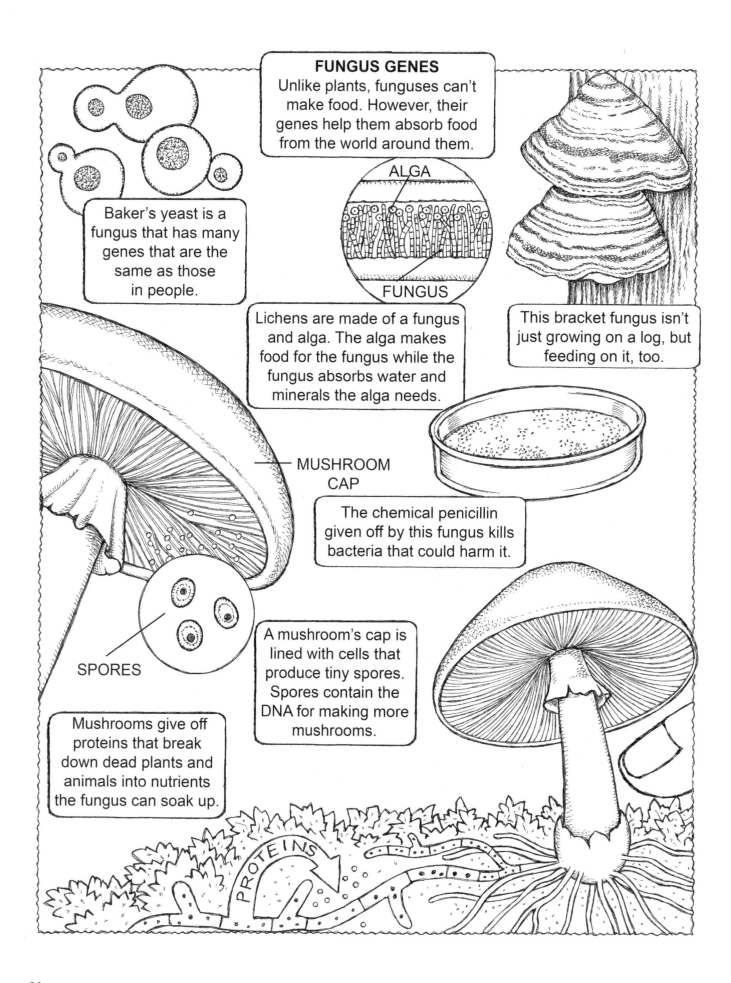

FUNGUS GENES
Unlike plants, funguses can't make food. However, their genes help them absorb food from the world around them.

ALGA

FUNGUS

Baker's yeast is a fungus that has many genes that are the same as those in people.

Lichens are made of a fungus and alga. The alga makes food for the fungus while the fungus absorbs water and minerals the alga needs.

This bracket fungus isn't just growing on a log, but feeding on it, too.

MUSHROOM CAP

The chemical penicillin given off by this fungus kills bacteria that could harm it.

SPORES

A mushroom's cap is lined with cells that produce tiny spores. Spores contain the DNA for making more mushrooms.

Mushrooms give off proteins that break down dead plants and animals into nutrients the fungus can soak up.

PROTEINS

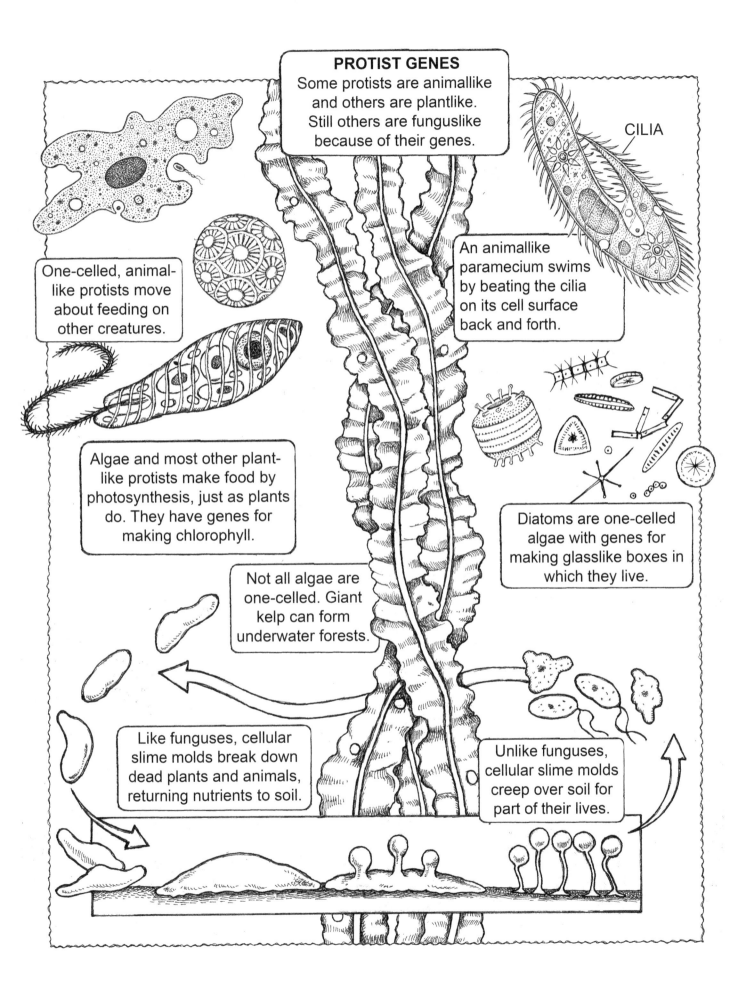

PROTIST GENES
Some protists are animallike and others are plantlike. Still others are funguslike because of their genes.

CILIA

One-celled, animal-like protists move about feeding on other creatures.

An animallike paramecium swims by beating the cilia on its cell surface back and forth.

Algae and most other plant-like protists make food by photosynthesis, just as plants do. They have genes for making chlorophyll.

Diatoms are one-celled algae with genes for making glasslike boxes in which they live.

Not all algae are one-celled. Giant kelp can form underwater forests.

Like funguses, cellular slime molds break down dead plants and animals, returning nutrients to soil.

Unlike funguses, cellular slime molds creep over soil for part of their lives.

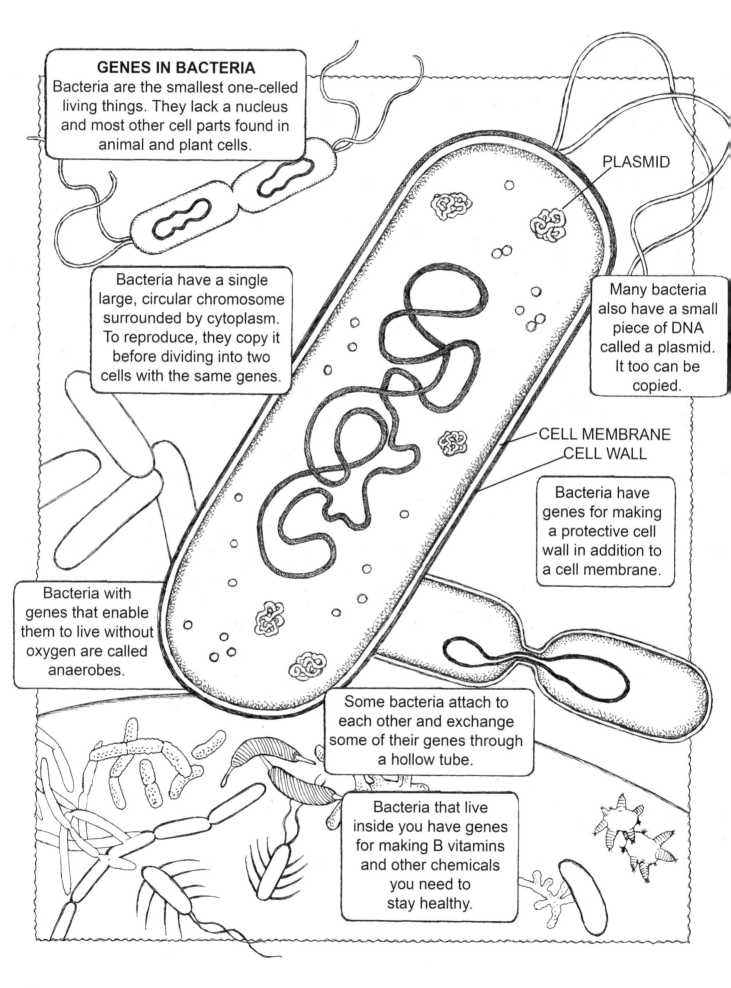

GENES IN BACTERIA
Bacteria are the smallest one-celled living things. They lack a nucleus and most other cell parts found in animal and plant cells.

PLASMID

Bacteria have a single large, circular chromosome surrounded by cytoplasm. To reproduce, they copy it before dividing into two cells with the same genes.

Many bacteria also have a small piece of DNA called a plasmid. It too can be copied.

CELL MEMBRANE
CELL WALL

Bacteria have genes for making a protective cell wall in addition to a cell membrane.

Bacteria with genes that enable them to live without oxygen are called anaerobes.

Some bacteria attach to each other and exchange some of their genes through a hollow tube.

Bacteria that live inside you have genes for making B vitamins and other chemicals you need to stay healthy.

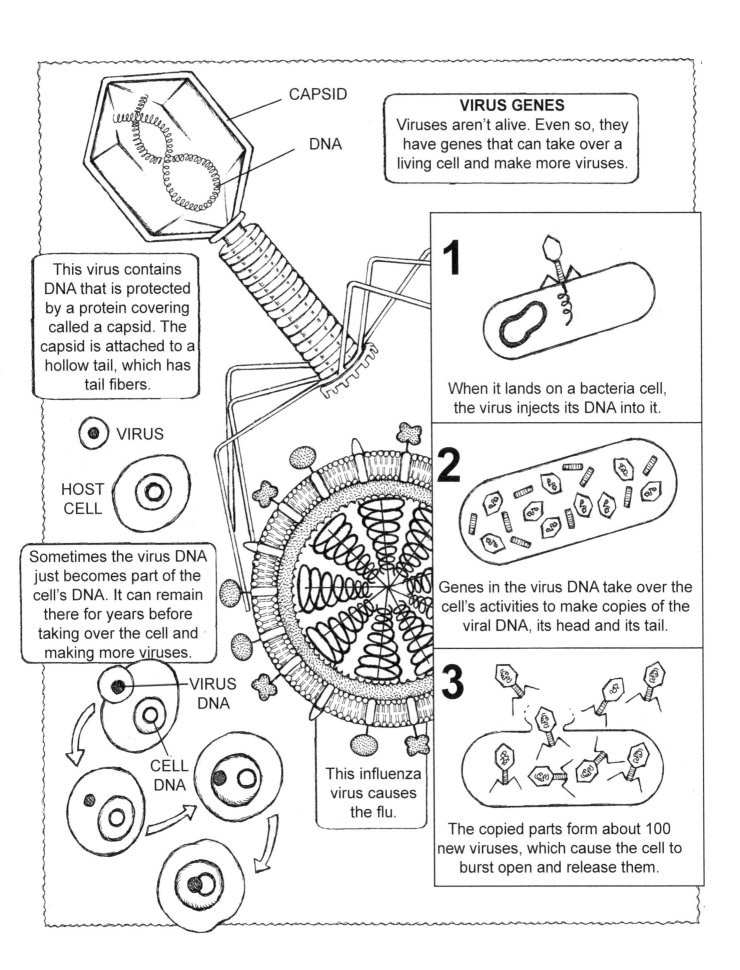

CAPSID

DNA

VIRUS GENES
Viruses aren't alive. Even so, they have genes that can take over a living cell and make more viruses.

This virus contains DNA that is protected by a protein covering called a capsid. The capsid is attached to a hollow tail, which has tail fibers.

◉ VIRUS

HOST CELL

Sometimes the virus DNA just becomes part of the cell's DNA. It can remain there for years before taking over the cell and making more viruses.

VIRUS DNA

CELL DNA

This influenza virus causes the flu.

1
When it lands on a bacteria cell, the virus injects its DNA into it.

2
Genes in the virus DNA take over the cell's activities to make copies of the viral DNA, its head and its tail.

3
The copied parts form about 100 new viruses, which cause the cell to burst open and release them.

NEW COMBINATIONS OF GENES AND CHROMOSOMES

Meiosis is the process that makes sperm and egg cells. During meiosis, special cells divide twice and new gene combinations form.

3

The chromosomes are copied, making 16 in total. The copies are held together at the centromere.

Female   Male

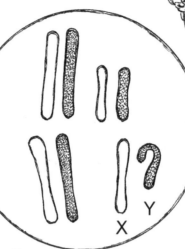

X   Y

1

This male fruit fly has 8 chromosomes in its body cells.

2

Chromosomes have the same kinds of genes in the same places. The X and Y are sex chromosomes.

6

The cell divides into two cells, each with 8 chromosomes. Some chromosomes have new combinations of genes.

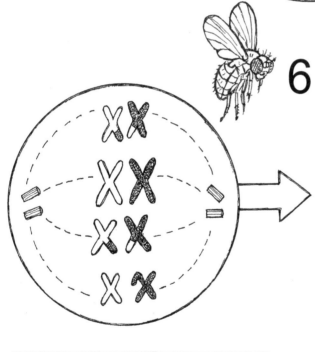

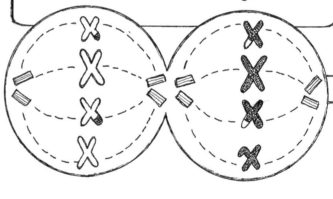

8

Four cells form, each with 4 chromosomes—half the original number. The cells are not the same—they have different combinations of chromosomes and genes.

4

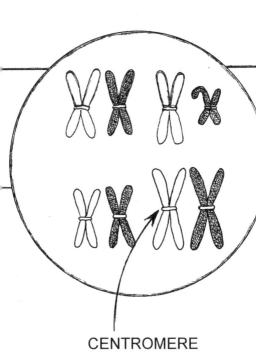

CENTROMERE

In the first part of meiosis, four sets of chromosomes move next to each other. So do the X and Y.

5

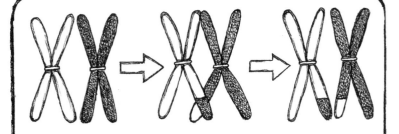

Breaks can open up in the same spots on the chromosome pairs. The broken parts can cross over and swap genes. Then the breaks close.

NEW GENE COMBINATIONS
In the second part of meiosis, the chromosomes are NOT copied again.

7

Fibers pull apart the chromosomes as each cell divides.

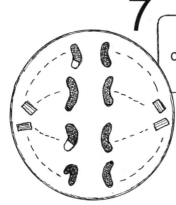

When the male fruit fly mates with a female, one sperm unites with one egg. The full number of chromosomes is restored—half from the male and half from the female.

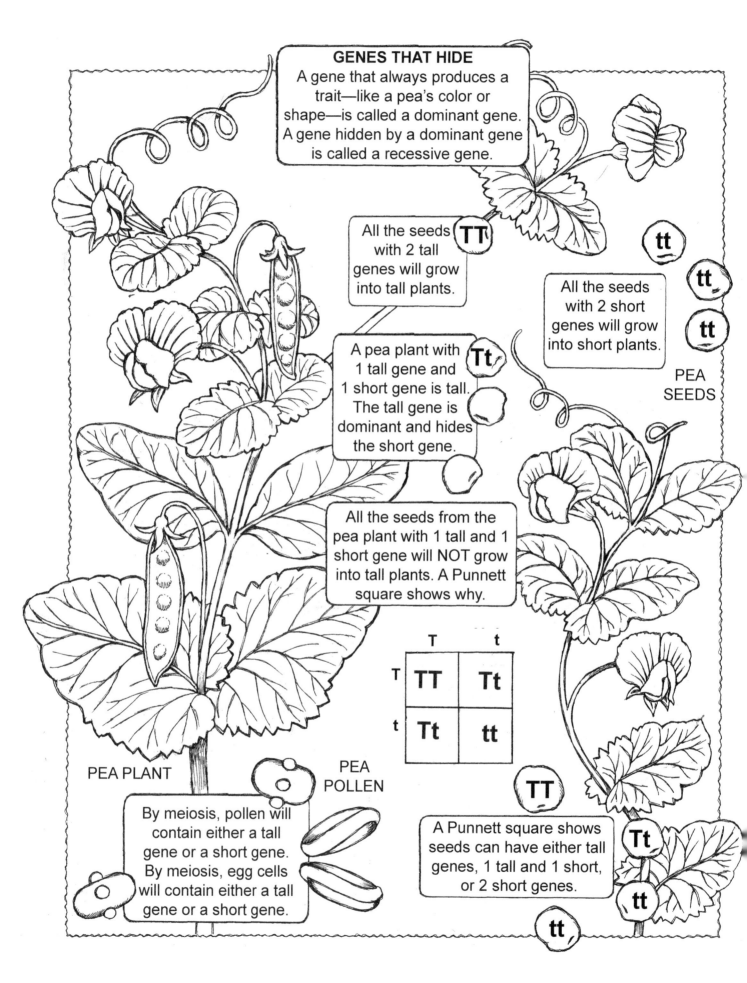

GENES THAT HIDE
A gene that always produces a trait—like a pea's color or shape—is called a dominant gene. A gene hidden by a dominant gene is called a recessive gene.

All the seeds with 2 tall genes will grow into tall plants.

All the seeds with 2 short genes will grow into short plants.

A pea plant with 1 tall gene and 1 short gene is tall. The tall gene is dominant and hides the short gene.

All the seeds from the pea plant with 1 tall and 1 short gene will NOT grow into tall plants. A Punnett square shows why.

PEA SEEDS

	T	t
T	TT	Tt
t	Tt	tt

PEA PLANT

PEA POLLEN

By meiosis, pollen will contain either a tall gene or a short gene. By meiosis, egg cells will contain either a tall gene or a short gene.

A Punnett square shows seeds can have either tall genes, 1 tall and 1 short, or 2 short genes.

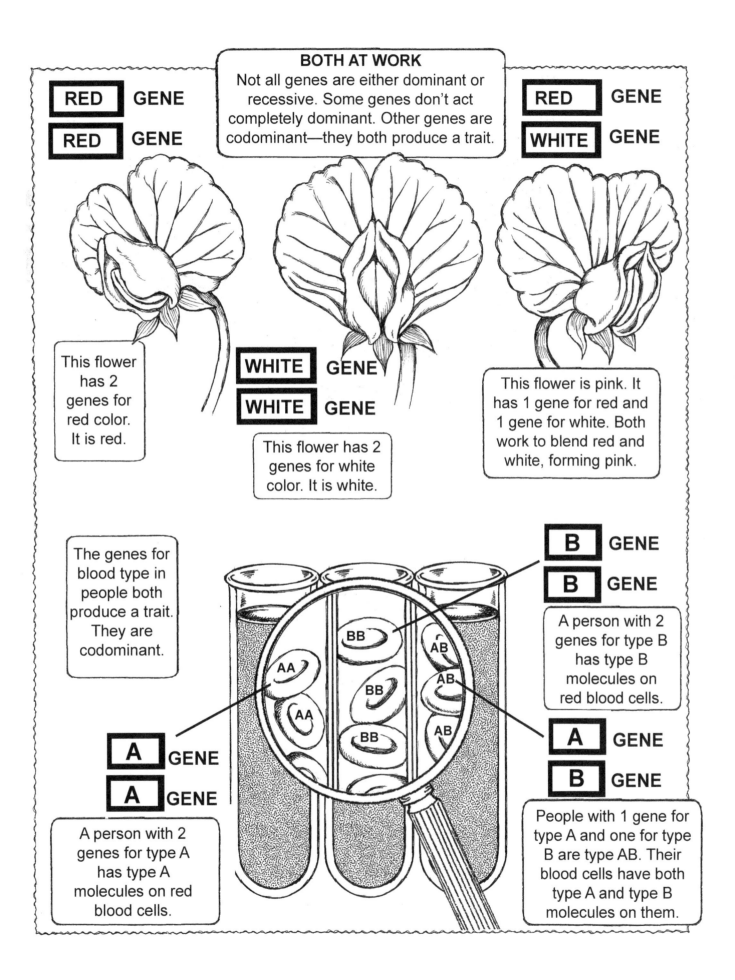

RED GENE
RED GENE

BOTH AT WORK
Not all genes are either dominant or recessive. Some genes don't act completely dominant. Other genes are codominant—they both produce a trait.

RED GENE
WHITE GENE

This flower has 2 genes for red color. It is red.

WHITE GENE
WHITE GENE

This flower has 2 genes for white color. It is white.

This flower is pink. It has 1 gene for red and 1 gene for white. Both work to blend red and white, forming pink.

B GENE
B GENE

The genes for blood type in people both produce a trait. They are codominant.

A person with 2 genes for type B has type B molecules on red blood cells.

A GENE
B GENE

A GENE
A GENE

A person with 2 genes for type A has type A molecules on red blood cells.

People with 1 gene for type A and one for type B are type AB. Their blood cells have both type A and type B molecules on them.

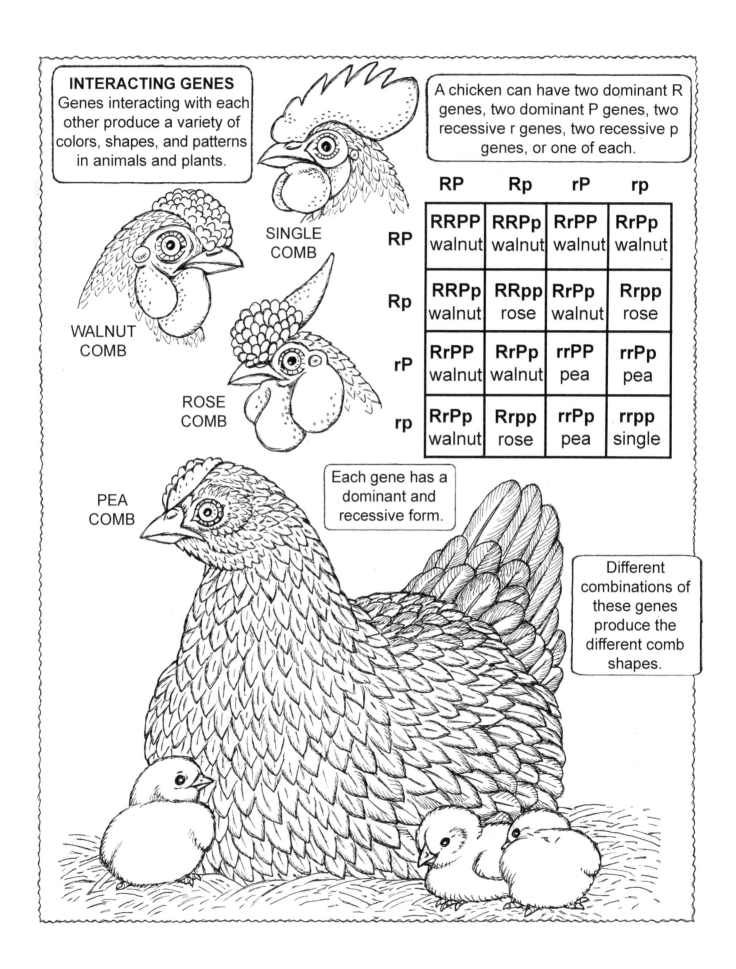

INTERACTING GENES
Genes interacting with each other produce a variety of colors, shapes, and patterns in animals and plants.

A chicken can have two dominant R genes, two dominant P genes, two recessive r genes, two recessive p genes, or one of each.

SINGLE COMB

WALNUT COMB

ROSE COMB

PEA COMB

	RP	Rp	rP	rp
RP	**RRPP** walnut	**RRPp** walnut	**RrPP** walnut	**RrPp** walnut
Rp	**RRPp** walnut	**RRpp** rose	**RrPp** walnut	**Rrpp** rose
rP	**RrPP** walnut	**RrPp** walnut	**rrPP** pea	**rrPp** pea
rp	**RrPp** walnut	**Rrpp** rose	**rrPp** pea	**rrpp** single

Each gene has a dominant and recessive form.

Different combinations of these genes produce the different comb shapes.

MASKING THE COLOR
Labrador Retriever dogs can be black, brown, or golden yellow. Their fur color is controlled by two different genes.

One of the genes has two forms, producing either black fur or brown. Black (B) is dominant over brown (b).

B GENE
b GENE

E GENE
The other gene also has two forms. One gene (E) allows the black or brown color in the fur.

e GENE
The other gene (e) masks the black or brown color, leaving the fur golden yellow.

BLACK DOG

BROWN DOG

YELLOW DOG

One gene masking or stopping the effects of a different gene is called epistasis.

CALICO CATS
Did you ever see a calico cat? It has patches of orange, black, and white fur. And the cat is almost always female.

There are two forms of sex chromosomes: X and Y. Females have two X chromosomes; males have an X and a Y.

In every cell of a female cat's body one of the X chromosomes is shut down so it cannot do its job.

FEMALE X CHROMOSOMES

BLACK

ORANGE

SHUT DOWN

In calico cats, there are two forms of a fur color gene on the X chromosome—black and orange.

Orange fur patches mean the X chromosome gene for black fur is shut down.

CALICO CAT

The patches of white fur come from a gene on another chromosome that hides the orange and black colors.

Black fur patches mean the X chromosome gene for orange fur is shut down.

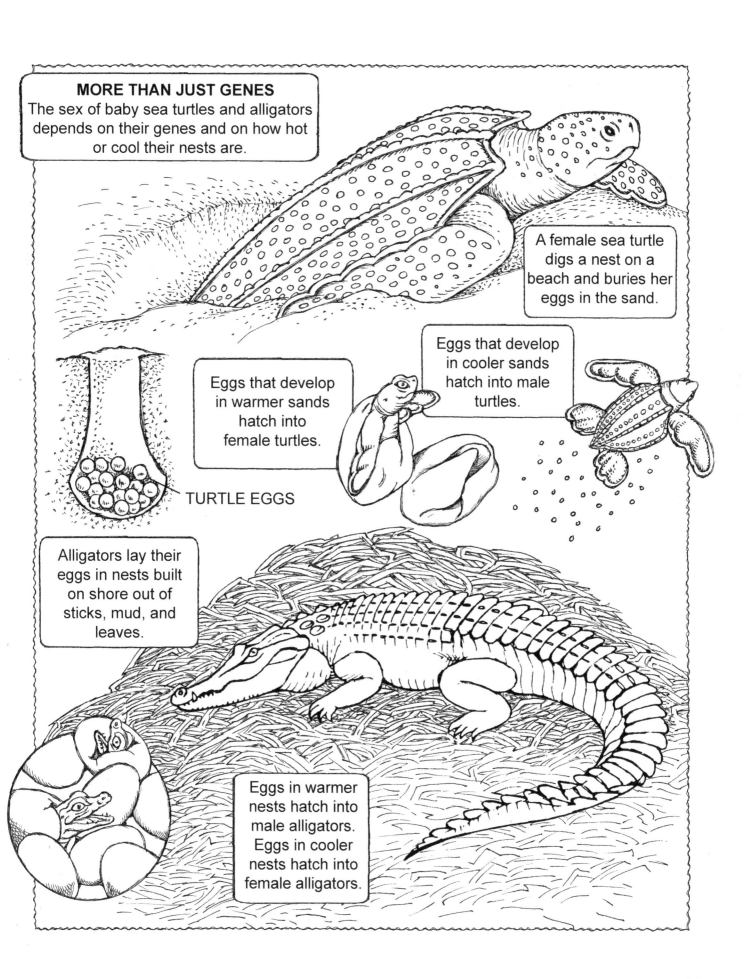

MORE THAN JUST GENES
The sex of baby sea turtles and alligators depends on their genes and on how hot or cool their nests are.

A female sea turtle digs a nest on a beach and buries her eggs in the sand.

Eggs that develop in warmer sands hatch into female turtles.

TURTLE EGGS

Eggs that develop in cooler sands hatch into male turtles.

Alligators lay their eggs in nests built on shore out of sticks, mud, and leaves.

Eggs in warmer nests hatch into male alligators. Eggs in cooler nests hatch into female alligators.

31

ORDER, ORDER

The order of the chemical code in genes is the key to making proteins. But the order of some groups of genes called homeobox or HOX genes is just as important. Animals' HOX genes control where body parts grow.

HOX genes switch other genes on or off, making sure the genes do their jobs at the right time and in the right way.

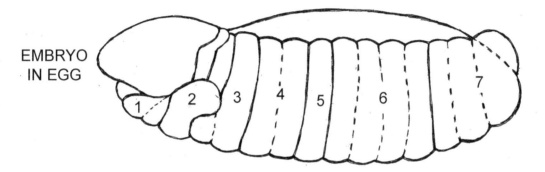

| HEAD | MOUTH | LEG 1 | LEG 2 AND THORAX | LEG 3 AND THORAX | SEGMENTS OF THE ABDOMEN 1–4 5–8 |

HOX GENES

EMBRYO IN EGG

As a new fruit fly develops inside its egg, its body becomes divided into sections.

The order of the HOX genes in its DNA is the same as the order of the sections from the fly's head to its tail.

A change in a HOX gene can result in a fly with legs growing out of its head! Any change in DNA is called a mutation.

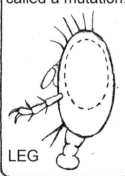

LEG

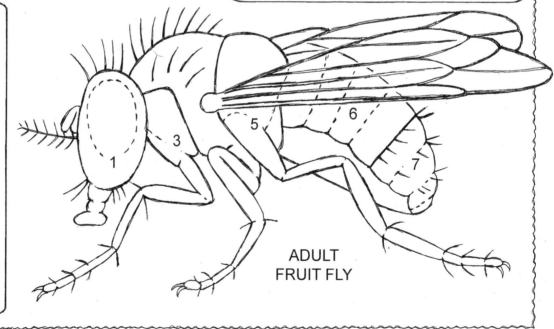

ADULT FRUIT FLY

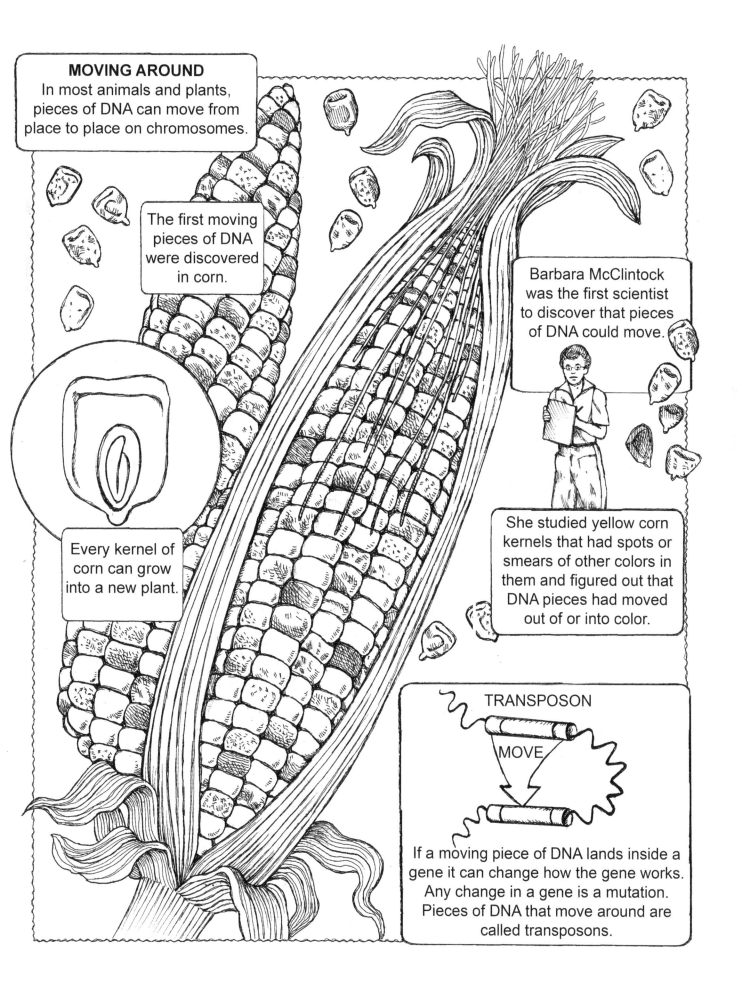

MOVING AROUND
In most animals and plants, pieces of DNA can move from place to place on chromosomes.

The first moving pieces of DNA were discovered in corn.

Barbara McClintock was the first scientist to discover that pieces of DNA could move.

Every kernel of corn can grow into a new plant.

She studied yellow corn kernels that had spots or smears of other colors in them and figured out that DNA pieces had moved out of or into color.

TRANSPOSON

MOVE

If a moving piece of DNA lands inside a gene it can change how the gene works. Any change in a gene is a mutation. Pieces of DNA that move around are called transposons.

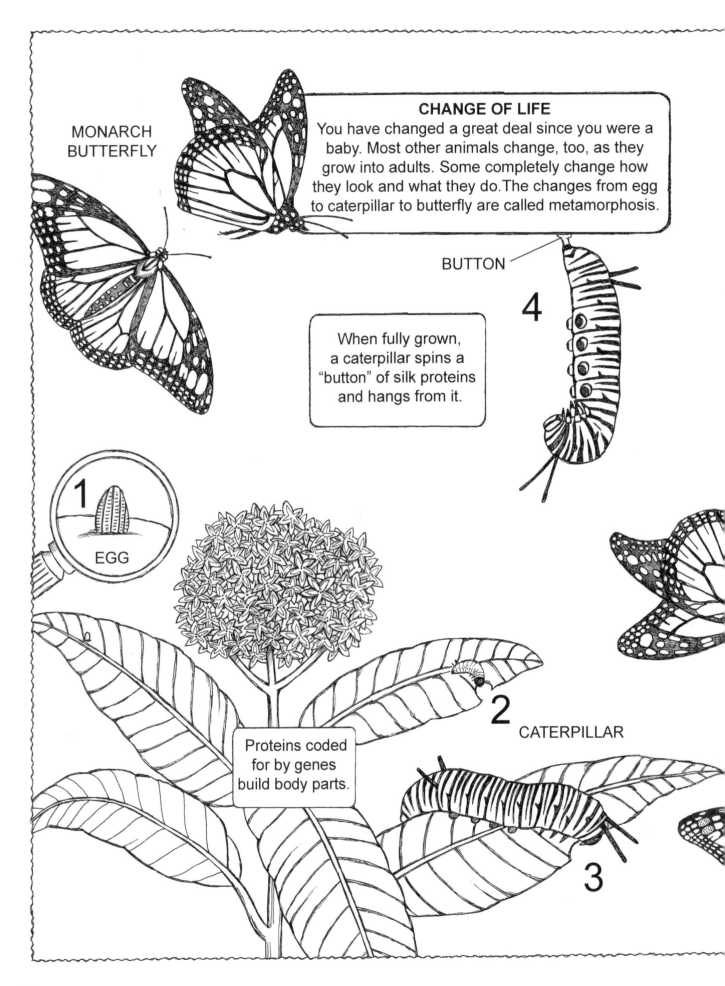

MONARCH
BUTTERFLY

CHANGE OF LIFE
You have changed a great deal since you were a baby. Most other animals change, too, as they grow into adults. Some completely change how they look and what they do. The changes from egg to caterpillar to butterfly are called metamorphosis.

BUTTON

4

When fully grown, a caterpillar spins a "button" of silk proteins and hangs from it.

1

EGG

Proteins coded for by genes build body parts.

2

CATERPILLAR

3

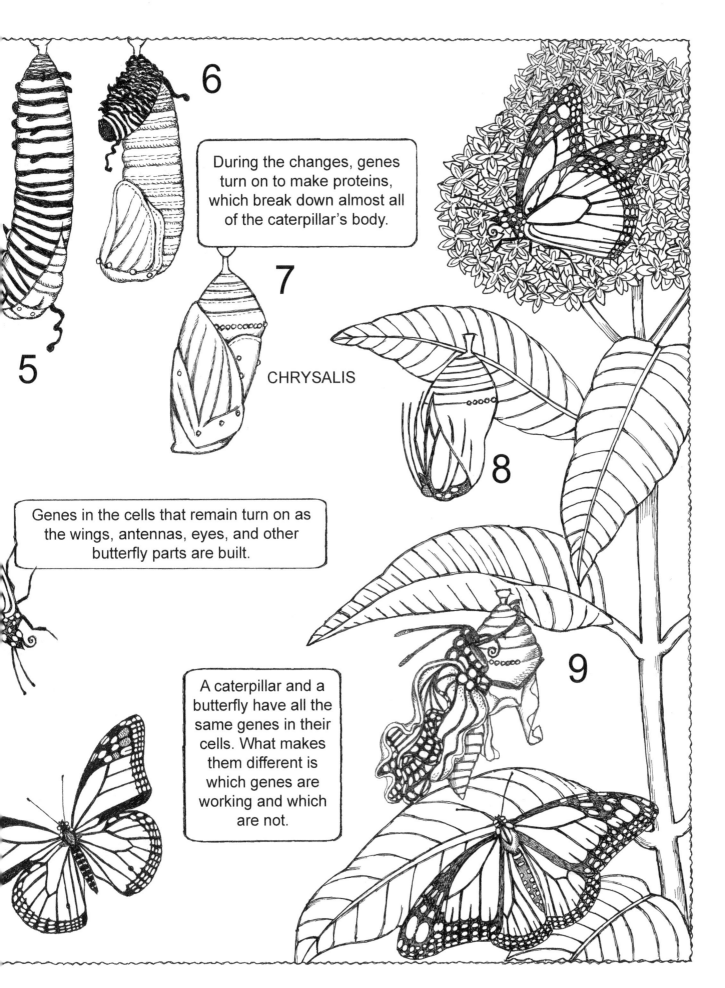

6

During the changes, genes turn on to make proteins, which break down almost all of the caterpillar's body.

7

5

CHRYSALIS

8

Genes in the cells that remain turn on as the wings, antennas, eyes, and other butterfly parts are built.

9

A caterpillar and a butterfly have all the same genes in their cells. What makes them different is which genes are working and which are not.

FROM EGG TO YOU
You started out as a fertilized egg cell inside your mother's body. This means that 23 chromosomes from your father joined with 23 chromosomes from your mother to form you.

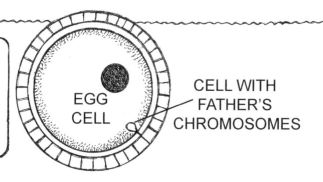

EGG CELL

CELL WITH FATHER'S CHROMOSOMES

After fertilization, the egg cell divided into smaller and smaller cells.

 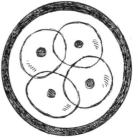 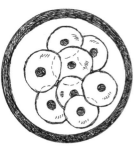 

Three cell layers formed. Cells in each layer turned on different genes that built different body parts.

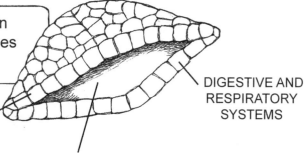

DIGESTIVE AND RESPIRATORY SYSTEMS

HAIR, NERVOUS SYSTEM, EARS, NOSE, AND EYES

MUSCLES, BONES, CARTILAGE, KIDNEYS, BLOOD AND CIRCULATORY SYSTEM

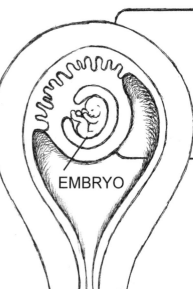

EMBRYO

By the end of the first month you were no bigger than a pea. Genes were developing your brain and other parts of your nervous system.

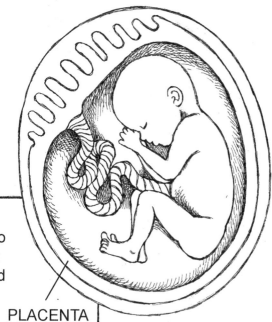

A ropelike umbilical cord connected you to the placenta, so that you received food and oxygen from your mother's blood.

PLACENTA

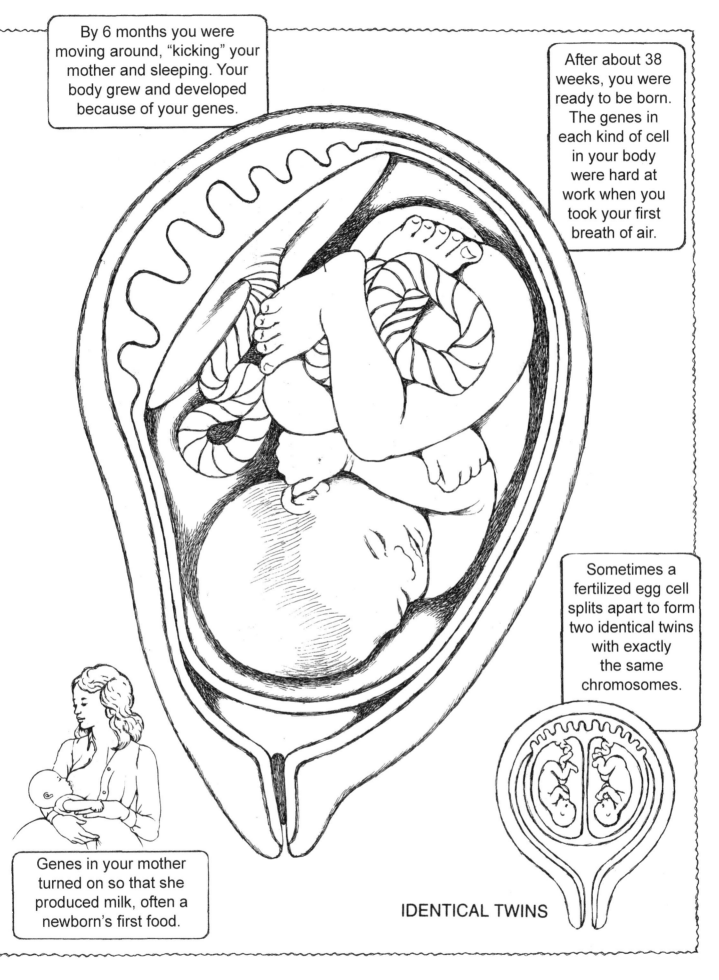

By 6 months you were moving around, "kicking" your mother and sleeping. Your body grew and developed because of your genes.

After about 38 weeks, you were ready to be born. The genes in each kind of cell in your body were hard at work when you took your first breath of air.

Sometimes a fertilized egg cell splits apart to form two identical twins with exactly the same chromosomes.

IDENTICAL TWINS

Genes in your mother turned on so that she produced milk, often a newborn's first food.

HARD TO TELL APART
When does a rabbit look like a fish? When does a chick look like a tortoise or a human baby? They all look alike in the early stages of life.

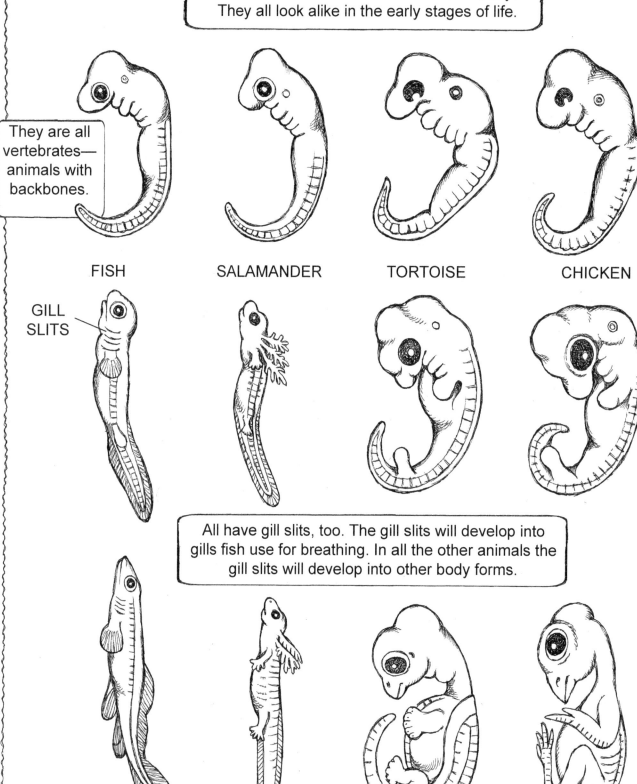

They are all vertebrates—animals with backbones.

FISH SALAMANDER TORTOISE CHICKEN

GILL SLITS

All have gill slits, too. The gill slits will develop into gills fish use for breathing. In all the other animals the gill slits will develop into other body forms.

As they develop further, a tortoise grows a shell while a chick loses most of its tail. A rabbit has a short tail while a human has none.

38

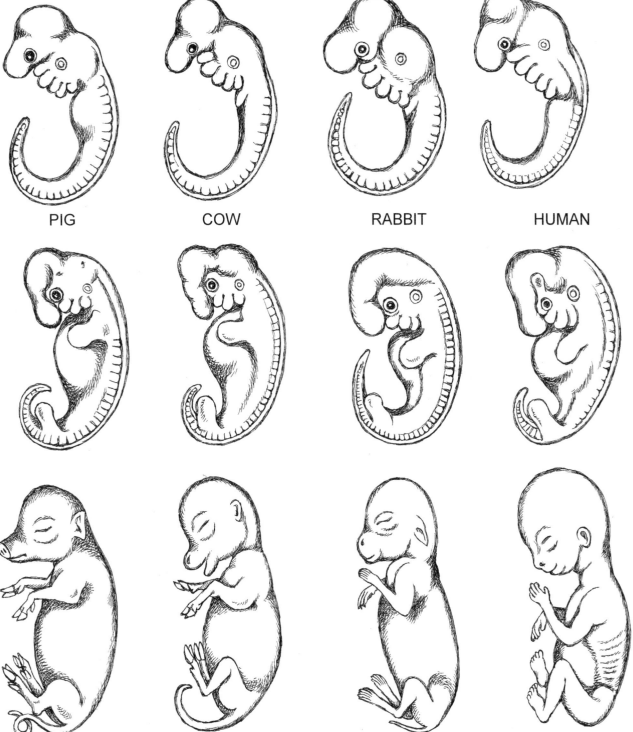

As they begin to develop from their fertilized eggs, fish, tortoises, chicks, rabbits, and humans all have eyes and tails and are hard to tell apart.

PIG   COW   RABBIT   HUMAN

By the time each animal is fully developed, its body parts have formed according to the chemical instructions contained in the genes it received from its parents.

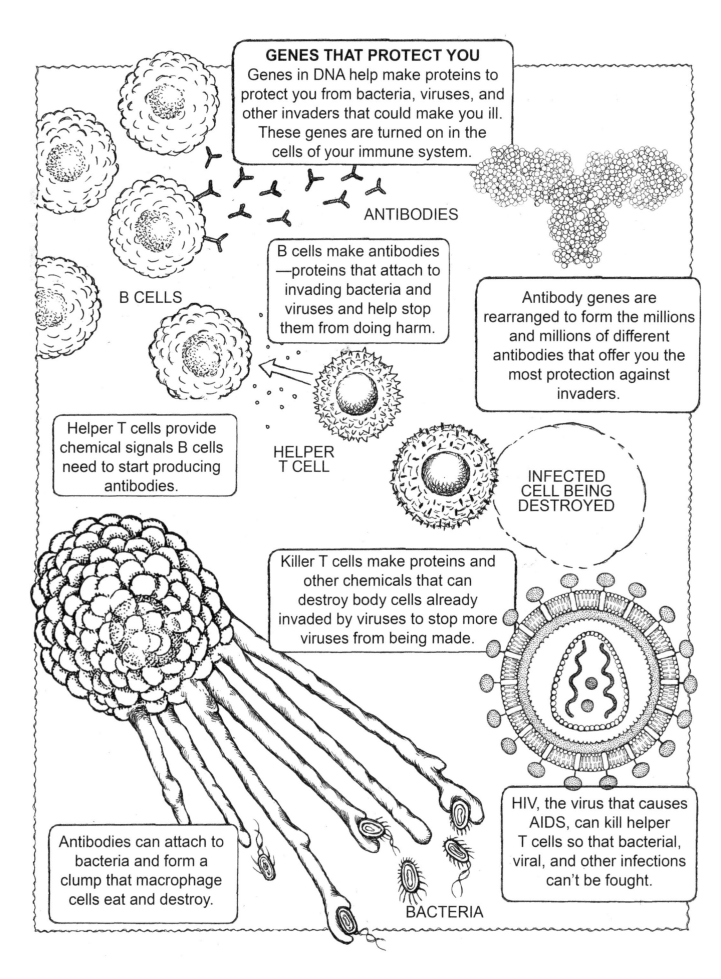

GENES THAT PROTECT YOU
Genes in DNA help make proteins to protect you from bacteria, viruses, and other invaders that could make you ill. These genes are turned on in the cells of your immune system.

ANTIBODIES

B CELLS

B cells make antibodies —proteins that attach to invading bacteria and viruses and help stop them from doing harm.

Antibody genes are rearranged to form the millions and millions of different antibodies that offer you the most protection against invaders.

Helper T cells provide chemical signals B cells need to start producing antibodies.

HELPER T CELL

INFECTED CELL BEING DESTROYED

Killer T cells make proteins and other chemicals that can destroy body cells already invaded by viruses to stop more viruses from being made.

Antibodies can attach to bacteria and form a clump that macrophage cells eat and destroy.

HIV, the virus that causes AIDS, can kill helper T cells so that bacterial, viral, and other infections can't be fought.

BACTERIA

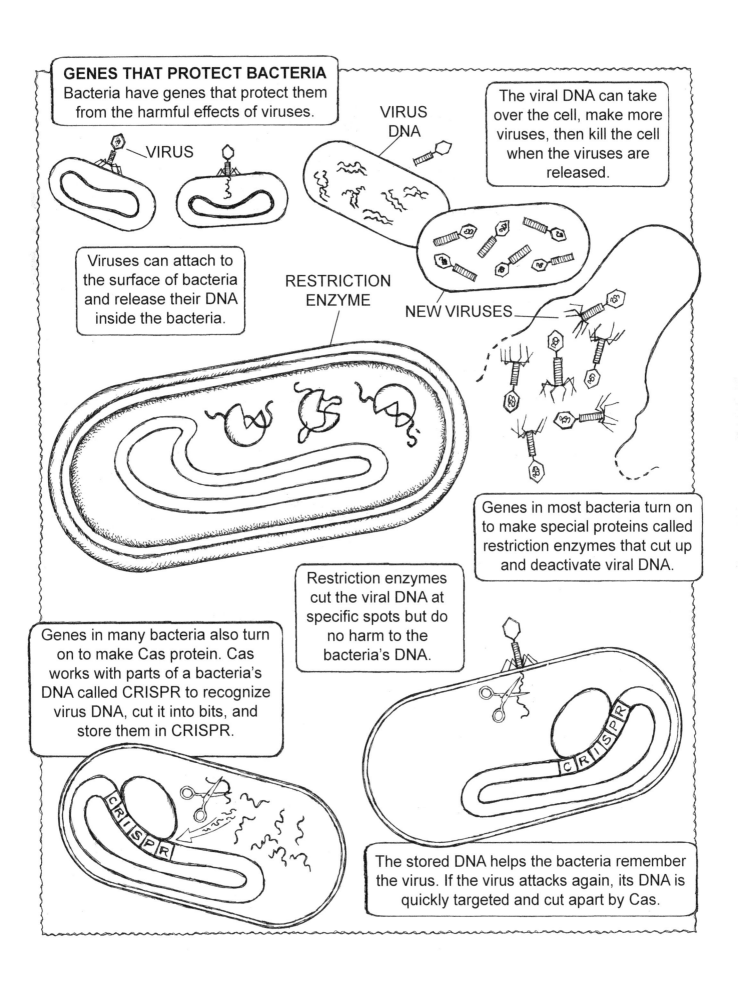

GENES THAT PROTECT BACTERIA
Bacteria have genes that protect them from the harmful effects of viruses.

VIRUS

VIRUS DNA

The viral DNA can take over the cell, make more viruses, then kill the cell when the viruses are released.

Viruses can attach to the surface of bacteria and release their DNA inside the bacteria.

RESTRICTION ENZYME

NEW VIRUSES

Genes in most bacteria turn on to make special proteins called restriction enzymes that cut up and deactivate viral DNA.

Restriction enzymes cut the viral DNA at specific spots but do no harm to the bacteria's DNA.

Genes in many bacteria also turn on to make Cas protein. Cas works with parts of a bacteria's DNA called CRISPR to recognize virus DNA, cut it into bits, and store them in CRISPR.

The stored DNA helps the bacteria remember the virus. If the virus attacks again, its DNA is quickly targeted and cut apart by Cas.

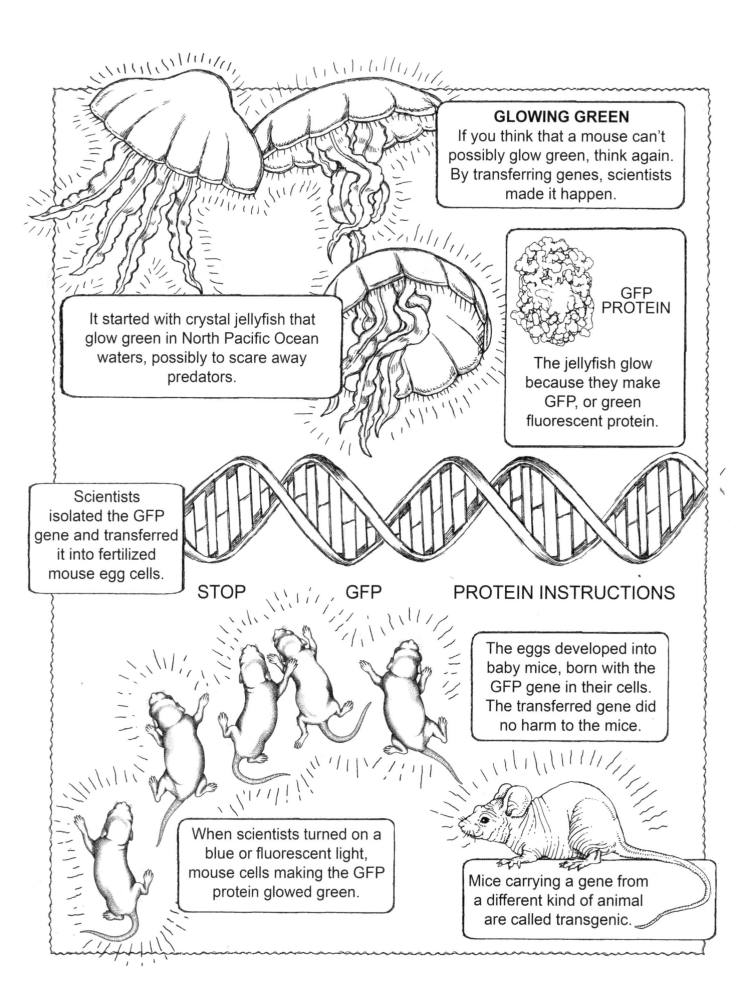

GLOWING GREEN
If you think that a mouse can't possibly glow green, think again. By transferring genes, scientists made it happen.

It started with crystal jellyfish that glow green in North Pacific Ocean waters, possibly to scare away predators.

GFP PROTEIN

The jellyfish glow because they make GFP, or green fluorescent protein.

Scientists isolated the GFP gene and transferred it into fertilized mouse egg cells.

STOP   GFP   PROTEIN INSTRUCTIONS

The eggs developed into baby mice, born with the GFP gene in their cells. The transferred gene did no harm to the mice.

When scientists turned on a blue or fluorescent light, mouse cells making the GFP protein glowed green.

Mice carrying a gene from a different kind of animal are called transgenic.

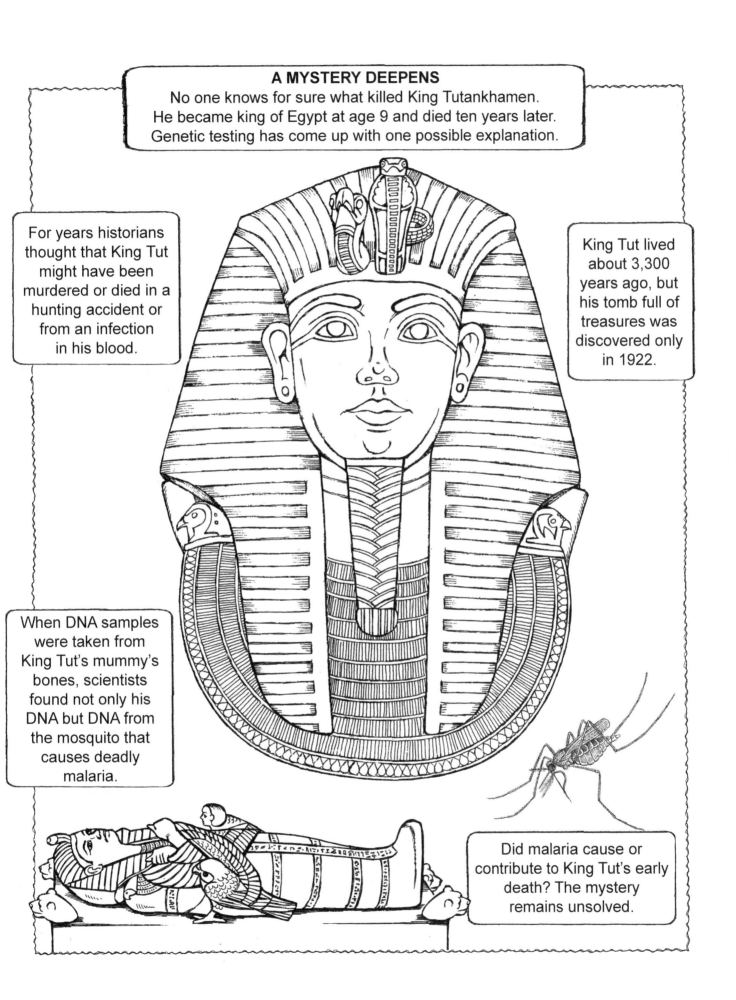

A MYSTERY DEEPENS
No one knows for sure what killed King Tutankhamen.
He became king of Egypt at age 9 and died ten years later.
Genetic testing has come up with one possible explanation.

For years historians thought that King Tut might have been murdered or died in a hunting accident or from an infection in his blood.

King Tut lived about 3,300 years ago, but his tomb full of treasures was discovered only in 1922.

When DNA samples were taken from King Tut's mummy's bones, scientists found not only his DNA but DNA from the mosquito that causes deadly malaria.

Did malaria cause or contribute to King Tut's early death? The mystery remains unsolved.

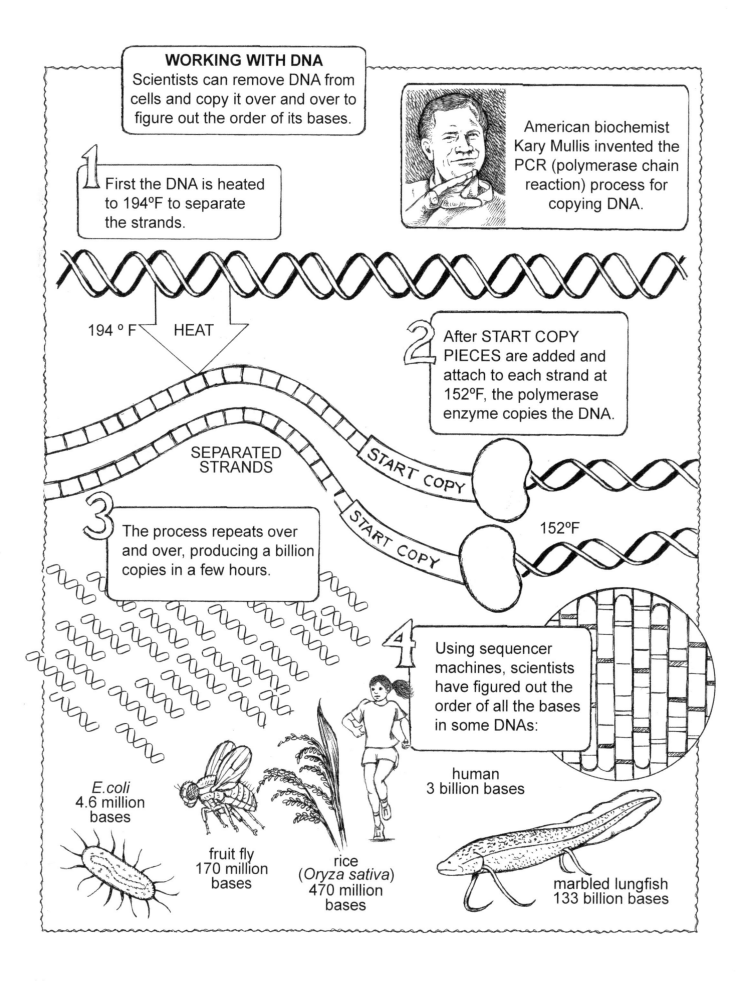

WORKING WITH DNA
Scientists can remove DNA from cells and copy it over and over to figure out the order of its bases.

American biochemist Kary Mullis invented the PCR (polymerase chain reaction) process for copying DNA.

1 First the DNA is heated to 194°F to separate the strands.

194° F   HEAT

2 After START COPY PIECES are added and attach to each strand at 152°F, the polymerase enzyme copies the DNA.

SEPARATED STRANDS

START COPY

START COPY

152°F

3 The process repeats over and over, producing a billion copies in a few hours.

4 Using sequencer machines, scientists have figured out the order of all the bases in some DNAs:

human 3 billion bases

E.coli 4.6 million bases

fruit fly 170 million bases

rice (*Oryza sativa*) 470 million bases

marbled lungfish 133 billion bases

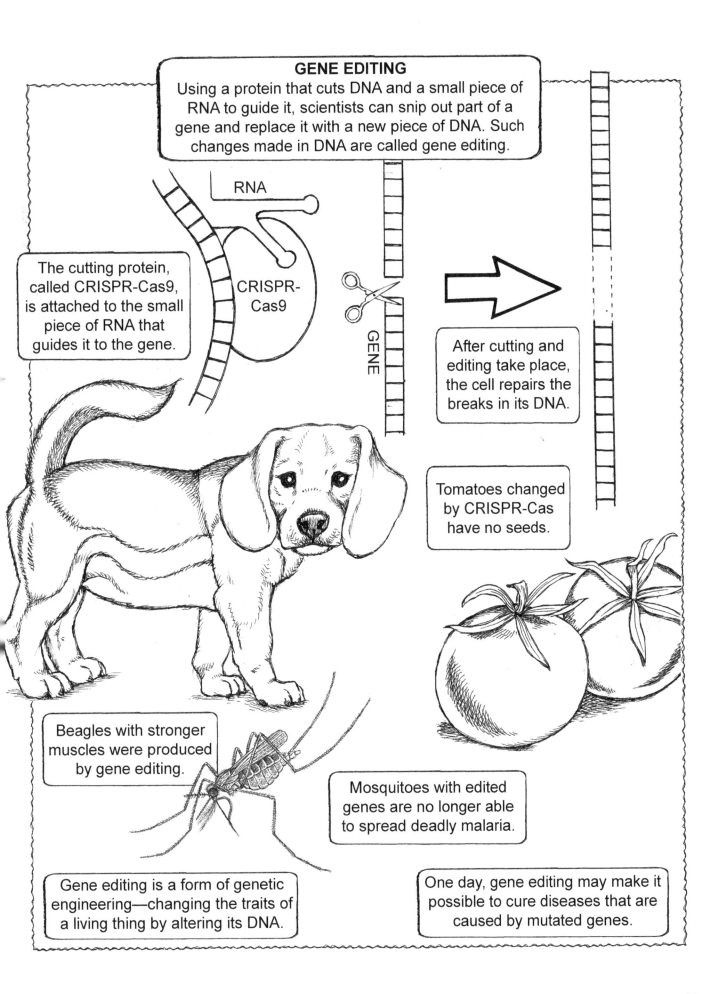

GENE EDITING
Using a protein that cuts DNA and a small piece of RNA to guide it, scientists can snip out part of a gene and replace it with a new piece of DNA. Such changes made in DNA are called gene editing.

RNA

The cutting protein, called CRISPR-Cas9, is attached to the small piece of RNA that guides it to the gene.

CRISPR-Cas9

GENE

After cutting and editing take place, the cell repairs the breaks in its DNA.

Tomatoes changed by CRISPR-Cas have no seeds.

Beagles with stronger muscles were produced by gene editing.

Mosquitoes with edited genes are no longer able to spread deadly malaria.

Gene editing is a form of genetic engineering—changing the traits of a living thing by altering its DNA.

One day, gene editing may make it possible to cure diseases that are caused by mutated genes.

45

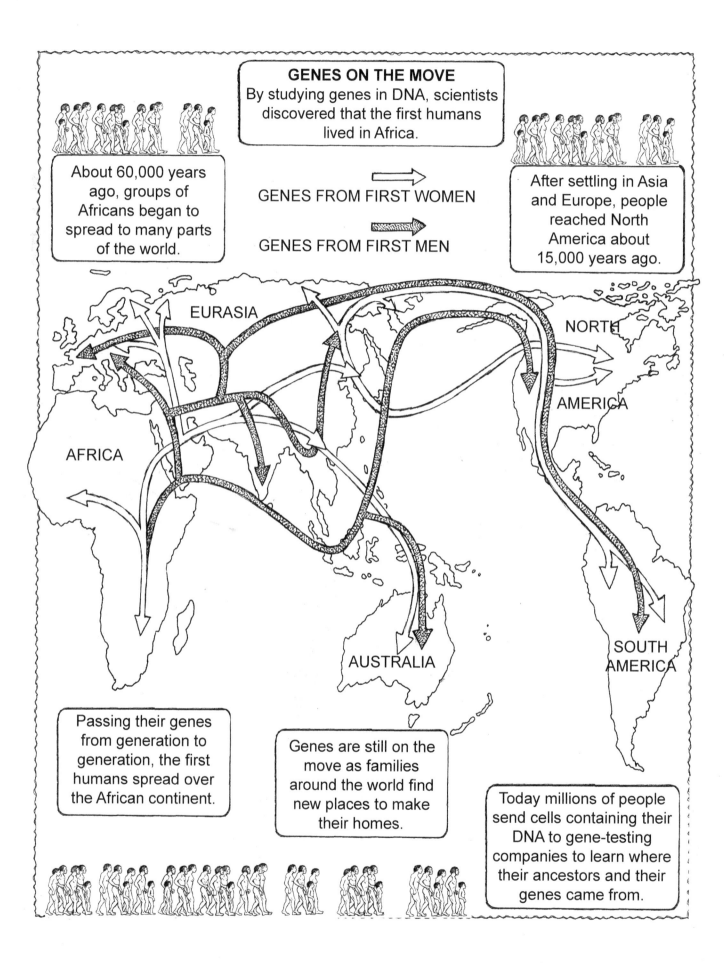